SHRAPNEL IN THE PIANO

Best wishes!

SHRAPNEL IN THE PIANO

A Family in Germany Before, During, and After WWII

B Nahmias

Brigitte "Bee" Buchmann Nahmias, MD

BOOKLOGIX®
Alpharetta, GA

Some names and identifying details have been changed to protect the privacy of individuals.

The author has tried to recreate events, locations, and conversations from his/her memories of them. In some instances, in order to maintain their anonymity, the author has changed the names of individuals and places. He/she may also have changed some identifying characteristics and details such as physical attributes, occupations, and places of residence.

ISBN: 978-1-63183-054-9
Library of Congress Control Number: 2016920021

10 9 8 7 6 5 4 3 2 1 2 2 8 1 6

Printed in the United States of America

∞ This paper meets the requirements of ANSI/NISO Z39.48-1992 (Permanence of Paper)

I dedicate this memoir to my mother, Klara Fueting Buchmann, and my father, Dr. Erich Buchmann.
Their love and care helped our family survive a terrible war with a positive spirit of courage and a strong sense of family.

I also dedicate this book to my wonderful children and grandchildren:

Cindy Nahmias Connor (Brad Connor) and Sean, Alex, and Olivia
David Nahmias (Cathy O'Neil Nahmias) and Steven and Michael
Eddy Nahmias (Cheryl Kopec Nahmias) and Lucas, Sam, and Eve

and to the generations to come.

"We lay aside letters never to read them again, and at last destroy them out of discretion, and so disappears the most beautiful, the most immediate breath of life, irrevocably for ourselves and for others."

—Johann Wolfgang von Goethe (1749–1832)

CONTENTS

Preface

Much has been written about World War II and the years preceding and following it. Readers and writers generally are aware that, throughout the ages, most history is spoken, written, and pictured from the victors' points of view.

This book is different. It is not a novel, not a military or political history, not a holocaust story. Rather, it is a story about a family that lived through that dreadful war in Germany. Books about World War II are very popular, but few describe life during that time from the point of view of a German family with children.

I have written this memoir as an elder, a mother of three, and a grandmother of eight in order to preserve memories. Our family was fortunate to have immigrated into the United States after the war in 1948. My parents were then in their forties, I was fifteen, and my brother was eleven. I went to BCC (Bethesda-Chevy Chase High School) in Bethesda, Maryland, then to college and medical school at GW (George Washington University) in Washington, DC, where I met and married my classmate, Andre Nahmias, a Sephardic Jewish student who had immigrated from Alexandria, Egypt. We settled in Atlanta, Georgia, and had three children. They've grown up to be successful and happy. After thirty years, Andy and I divorced amicably. My second husband, Don Norton, was a professional classical musician. My greatest pleasures in retired life now are family, medicine, activities with friends, listening to music, playing piano and recorders, gardening, reading, and travel.

My book is based on rich and contemporary source material which I found, after my parents died, in six boxes of letters, photo albums, diaries, and documents. Much of the book comes directly from my mother's writings and reflects her point of view at the time.

Occasionally my own memories are interspersed, and once in a while I include some thoughts from my present, mature point of view.

It took ten years to translate all the letters and documents. I usually did this work during the summers, which Don and I spent on Crystal Lake, in Michigan.

The first part of this memoir begins when my parents met in Düsseldorf in 1929. Having lived through World War I in their teens, they started their young family in the bourgeois style of the time, with high hopes for their future and that they and their children would be living in peacetime. But rather quickly, Germans had to cope with a regime change to a fascist dictatorship under Adolf Hitler, resulting in the loss of many civil rights, such as freedom of speech, press, and assembly. A few years later, in 1939, World War II befell them.

In the second part of the memoir, I describe how our family coped with the terrible times during the most destructive war in history, in which more civilians died worldwide than military personnel. Civilians died from bombings, displacements, starvation, and disease, as well as in prisons, concentration camps, and gulags. Terror was consciously and specifically aimed at civilian targets through air raids, with the aim of discouraging the population. This was true for both the Axis and the Allies. Germans bombed London and other British cities. British and Americans bombed Berlin and other German cities, and Americans used two atomic bombs over Japan.

I describe how my parents worked hard to protect us children and spare us as much knowledge of the war's dangers as possible. They tried never to talk about the war in my or my brother's presence and strived to maintain a normal sense of family life despite all the disruptions and displacements. This memoir is also the story of how children experience war with the terror of air raids; with evacuations; with the extreme shortages of food, coal, clothing, paper, and other materials; and of course the absence of luxury items. It is a story of endurance and courage with a spirit of resilience and survival. It also becomes clear that children take life as it is, with a matter-of-fact attitude. Parents have a much harder time.

The third part of this memoir describes the years after the war, which were very difficult for most Germans. It was unusually cold, and food and fuel were extremely scarce. The cities lay in rubble and yet there were about ten million refugees from the eastern, Soviet-occupied portions of the former Germany who streamed into these cities, seeking shelter and help. Millions of people died. The final defeat, demanding unconditional surrender after this second war in just thirty years, left Germans demoralized. In addition, blame for the war and for the abominations of the concentration camps was laid on the entire German population.

This memoir is a gift not only to my family, but also to other families, to historians looking for primary source material, to departments of studies of German culture and language, and to physicians and psychologists studying the effects of war and trauma on children and adults. Departments of social studies, women's studies, and behavioral sciences may also be interested.

The book may be especially interesting for Americans of German descent. They are more numerous than I realized. The 2000 census listed 49 to 50 million people who noted German ancestry, making this the largest single ethnic group in the United States at that time. I was surprised also to learn that between 1820 and 1940 there were more immigrants from Germany than from any other country: 6,022,000. By comparison, there were 4,581,000 from Ireland; 4,719,000 from Italy; and 4,267,000 from the UK. Due to the two world wars, many German names of persons and places in the United States were changed.

I have often wondered why so little has been written and discussed about German families in World War II by persons who lived through it. I never spoke about my wartime childhood, not in high school, college, or medical school. I did not talk to my three children about it, while living a normal life as physician, wife, mother, PTA president, and soccer mom. My contemporaries did not talk about it. Neither did my parents and their contemporaries, most of whom have now died. We did not want to retrieve terrible emotions and memories, just as combat veterans and people who have experienced other severe trauma don't like to speak about it. My writing in this memoir is rather unemotional and matter of fact for the same reason. I think that on the whole, suppressing the bad memories served me well enough. However, I remember times I did experience very strong feelings of terror and sorrow. One such occasion was on September 11, 2001, when I heard on my car radio, "The United States is under attack." I felt panicked and quickly drove home and asked a friend to come over for tea and sympathy. Another unexpected episode happened when I heard a burglar alarm going off, which sounded like the howling sirens in my childhood. More recently I burst into unstoppable tears of fear, sorrow, and sympathy when viewing TV reports of mass school shootings. Obviously my earlier memories have not been erased, but rather they have been suppressed and subdued.

At least I spared my children and grandchildren the intimate and repeated information and knowledge of wartime realities, just as my parents spared us children as much as possible.

As matriarch of our family in the United States, and as an elder, I am happy to have fulfilled an obligation I have felt to preserve our family's German memories, which would otherwise have been lost forever. I am proud of my children and grandchildren and of what we have achieved in this wonderful land of opportunity.

ACKNOWLEDGMENTS

So many kind people have helped me with this memoir that I'm sure I'll forget to mention someone, especially since it took so long to complete the task. I hope I'll be forgiven, since memory is frail. Just translating all the documents from German into English took over ten years, since I only had some time during summer vacations to do it. In this respect my aunt Maria Buchmann and my friend in Michigan, Ruth Budisic, were helpful, since they were able to read the old Sütterlin script of the letters of the late 1800s.

My children, Cindy Connor, David Nahmias, and Eddy Nahmias gave many helpful suggestions. Eddy and Cheryl, Eddy's wife, also helped me navigate Word.

My eight grandchildren, Sean, Alex, Olivia, Steven, Michael, Lucas, Sam, and Eve are, of course, the reason for all the work of translating, researching, sorting photos, and writing this memoir.

I attended several writing classes at Emory University's OLLI program (Osher Lifelong Learning Institute). This was very helpful to me, since most of my previous writing had been medical. Enid Griss and Audrey Galex taught memoir writing, and Bard Lindeman and Trudy Kretchman were role models for personal articles.

The UUCA (Unitarian Universalist Congregation of Atlanta) Women Writers were inspirational for several years, especially Lanie Damon; Janet Paulk; Kim Foster Green, author of *Hallucinations*; Sandy Gillespie; and Nina Gross.

Gladys Fletcher in Michigan critiqued my very first draft, and Linda Gadjusek my second one. Dirk Wales in Santa Fe, author of numerous films and books, was very encouraging and ordered two books in advance. Dr. Martin Buss explained the theology of the biblical Abraham. Aimee Wise gave me many helpful tips, which she had gleaned while publishing her memoir *Of Human Clay: The Making and Breaking of a Nun*. Hans and Sonia Prauser reviewed my book, and Hans gave me a copy of his own memoir *Unforeseen* (see Additional Reading). Roger Easley scanned all the photos in my mother's album.

I am grateful to my first husband, Dr. Andre Nahmias, for reviewing the manuscript and making many helpful comments. My second husband, Dr. Donald Norton, was the person who inspired me to write in the first place.

My German-speaking friends Dr. Angelika Pohl and Jule Schmidt kept my German fluent, and my closest friends, Marsha Jones and Mary Bartlett, were the engine that kept pushing me on all along. Mary came up with the title *Shrapnel in the Piano.*

The professional and attractive final product is the achievement of the editors and artists at BookLogix.

Introduction

Sitting in the kitchen of my trigenerational house, having lunch with my dear, long-term friends, Marsha Jones and Mary Bartlett, we hear my teenage grandson, Lucas, playing the piano upstairs.

It is a beautiful spinet piano, but it has metal shrapnel fragments and holes in it, all over the front and side. Nevertheless, it still plays well. This piano was my mother's, bought in Kiel, Germany, with joy and pride early in World War II, and it survived many moves, as well as a bombing. I want Lucas and all my family, and others, to know the story of this piano and of our family before, during, and after a terrible war. The piano is resilient, and so is my family. We survived the war, immigrated into the United States, and thrived. Marsha encouraged me over the years to write a family memoir. Mary had a flash of inspiration as we listened to the music and said, "Call the book *Shrapnel in the Piano*!"

My parents died rather suddenly in 1991, within three months of each other. It was a shock. Although they had reached the advanced ages of eighty-nine and eighty-seven, they had been in good health, and I was not prepared. My mother, Klara (KLAAH-rah), had a stroke, and my father, Erich (EH-rich), died of bowel obstruction. They had lived around the corner from my family and me for ten years and suddenly they were no longer there.

I remember walking with my brother to our parents' house and feeling very uneasy. It had been only two days since our father had died. He had felt lonely since his wife's death. Once he answered my phone call with "Lonesome Erich here." After all, Erich and Klara had been married for sixty-one years. I imagined that Klara had called him to join her, *"Ach Erich, komm doch schon!"* (Come on, Erich!)

My brother, Johnny Buchman, also a physician, had flown over from California to Atlanta for the memorial service. In my mind I still called him by his childhood nickname, Uli (OOL-lee), short for Ulrich (OOL-rich), but I was careful not to say it out loud because he didn't like it. Now he called himself Dr. Johnny Buchman (instead of Buchmann). We were going to the house to make arrangements for our parents' possessions.

Walking up the driveway, we saw their car in the carport. My eyes blurred with tears; my chest tightened up. Papa (PAH-pah) would never drive the blue Ford Taurus again. Opening the door to the kitchen, I felt like a sneak thief, intruding on Mutti's (MOOT-tee) and Papa's privacy. This was going to be very difficult.

Johnny looked at me. "Okay, Bee, where do we start?" He didn't use my childhood nickname—Gitte (GITT-ah), short for Brigitte (Bree-GITT-ah)—anymore either. It made me reflect that we've had many losses in our lives: our original nicknames, and our native country, language, and culture.

At first, we just wandered through the house, a three-bedroom ranch, and looked at all the rooms. It seemed unbelievable that our parents would never be here again. No longer would they sit at the kitchen table by the large picture window and wave at me and at neighbors whenever we drove by. No longer would my children sit at the table visiting with them, discussing their own interests: Cindy's in education, David's in law, and Eddy's in philosophy. No longer would their grandmother (Oma to them) hand out advice on life's problems while handing around a bowl of grapes to munch. No longer would their grandfather (Opa to them) give his well-considered opinions. And no longer would I often walk from my house, downhill and up around the curve of Vistavia Circle, to drop by unannounced. The emptiness overcame me and I had to sit down. "My goodness," I said to Johnny, "do you realize that now we're orphans?"

Finally, we started our task by looking at the furniture. Johnny did not want to transport anything large to California. I reserved Papa's big oak desk for myself and also Mutti's piano, still bearing shrapnel, but also still looking beautiful and playing well. I kept a few items for each of my children. The rest we decided to give to the German Lutheran Church for their refugee program. Next we divided the few jewelry pieces and then the lovely art-deco silver tableware. What to do with all the books? Johnny took a few and I decided to store the others in the basement of my house for now. And finally we tackled the papers. My father had kept meticulous financial records and made that part easy for us. But there were many, many other papers. We filled up six boxes, tightly packed. Johnny did not want them and I decided to put these in my basement also for now.

Too busy with final arrangements for the sale of the house and car after my brother flew home, and with my family, my work as a physician, with house and yard, friends, travel, and entertaining, I didn't look at these boxes any further.

It was not until four years later, in 1995, that I took another look. I had spent the summer with my new second husband, Don Norton, who had wanted to show me his hometown, Ludington, in Michigan. Don was also a doctor, but a doctor of classical music, who played violin, viola, and clarinet. While driving and walking, exploring the beautiful inland lakes and majestic Lake Michigan with its beaches, dunes, and lighthouses, Don told me story after story about his childhood and small-town upbringing. I suddenly became aware of how very, very different my own childhood had been. I had grown up with big-city life in Kiel and Berlin and other cities. But my family's life was disrupted by the air raid terror of World War II, evacuations, dislocations, the hard post-war years, and finally immigration into the United States, with the many adjustments to a new culture and language. For the first time a glimmer of interest in family history awoke in me, and when we returned home to Atlanta, I went downstairs to look at those boxes I'd stored.

What a treasure trove I found! Six boxes jam-packed with diaries, photo albums, letters, guest books, and documents. Almost everything was in German, of course. It struck me that I was now the matriarch of our family in America, and then I knew that I must preserve this material. My first task would be to translate everything into English. None of my children, or my brother, four years younger than I, knew German well enough. As I fingered through the papers, I even came across some letters handwritten by my maternal grandfather in the late 1800s and early 1900s, and these were written in the old "Gothic" Sütterlin script, which I couldn't read. A big task lay ahead of me, and I decided to do the translating during our summer vacations in Michigan.

The translations took many years and proved to be an exciting discovery. I learned about the courtship and early marriage years of my parents and also about their parents and other relatives, and I began to see them in a different light from my previous childhood perspective. I discovered events in my childhood that I had forgotten. I read about the war years and saw how my mother bravely held the family together and spared us children from too much specific knowledge and anxiety about the war. I read how my father protected us and found us safer places to live during the bombings.

I should write all this down and connect it, I thought. *The events, the family members and other people, customs of the time and how they changed, some political background, the terrors of the war, the struggle for survival, and the spirit of courage. I should write a book.* My husband, Don, agreed, and my first husband, Andy, later helped to edit the manuscript.

I took several writing and memoir courses at Emory University and joined the UUCA Women Writers group (Unitarian Universalist Congregation of Atlanta). This helped me to write in a different style from my usual medical professional one. I published several poems and stories, some in German and most in English. I also recently translated and published a children's booklet, which I originally had written and illustrated at age twelve for my brother near the end of the war.[1] During this learning time, I came across some words by Virginia Woolf that made an impression on me: "So much of written history is about politics, battles, military details and egos, mostly of men. If you ask what the experience of a woman or child has been, so often it is not remembered . . . For all the dinners are cooked; the plates and cups washed; the children set to school and gone out into the world. Nothing remains of it all. All has vanished. No biography or history has a word to say about it" (*A Room of One's Own*, 1929).

What follows is the story of our family in Germany in the pre-war years, during WWII, and in the post-war years. Much of the material is quoted directly and in quotation marks. I also filled in the story using audiotapes I transcribed from an oral history which my son, Eddy, took from my mother and father during the summer of 1988, three years before their deaths. I have added a few writings of my brother, when he was still very young, some of my own remembrances, and a few reflections of my later, more mature years.

---

[1] *Widdely, the Naughty Little Angel* (Alpharetta, GA: BookLogix, 2014). Available on amazon.com.

PART ONE

How Our Family Lived in Germany During the Pre-War Years

1929–1938

CHAPTER 1

1929: Klara and Erich Meet in Düsseldorf, Germany.

This chapter reads rather differently from all the subsequent ones in this book. That's because I took it almost verbatim from my mother, Klara's, diary. And for some reason, perhaps because she was a writer, she wrote this account of how she met Erich in the third person, as if she were writing a novel. I thought it was interesting when I first read these notes and have left them in this form. Some details were added from a series of interviews my teenage son, Eddy, conducted with my parents three years before they died.

She had noticed him before—a tall, well-built young man, one of the new physics professionals at the company. He was sitting with a group of other physicists at a large table in Frau Brünner's Restaurant, which billed itself with this slogan:

Hier kann man futtern	(Here you can munch
wie bei Muttern!	Mom's home-cooked lunch!)

This home cooking attracted a large crowd every day for the midday dinner, the main meal of the day. Klara Füting came here often with some of her coworkers from the large firm Rheinmetall, AG, in Düsseldorf, Germany. The company made steel products, especially huge construction cranes, which were exported worldwide. Klara was employed as a *Fremdsprachenkorrespondentin,* a trilingual corresponding secretary, comfortable in German, English, and French. It was a very good position for a young woman in 1929.

This was the year when the worldwide Great Depression began, the year of the New York Stock Exchange crash. Germany's government was the Weimar Republic, struggling with the aftermath of World War I

(1914–1918). An enormous war debt and uncontrollable hyperinflation were wiping out the entire savings of the middle class. Although the new constitution was very progressive, giving German women equal rights, the government was weak, with many parties disagreeing with each other, and there was painful unemployment and civil unrest.

Klara had managed to support herself for many years now and was proud of her accomplishments. She drew the second-highest salary of eighty women in the firm.

Talking across the table with a coworker, she said, "The food here really is great. We've got a good choice of meats and vegetables today. I think I'll get the pork roast, red cabbage, and peas, along with some boiled potatoes and gravy."

"And if I know you, you'll follow it up with a cup of strong coffee to keep you going for the afternoon," laughed her friend.

The atmosphere in the dining room was peaceful, until this new young man arrived. Klara overheard him criticizing a fellow researcher, who was reading the paper as he ate.

"In our family, this would be considered very bad manners!" he intoned.

Klara looked across the table disapprovingly. Her eyes met those of the disruptive physicist. She took in a bright-blue, smiling, responsive glance; Erich Buchmann, in turn, looked into her sparkling, challenging, and provocative hazel eyes.

Klara wrote in her diary that evening: "Everything was delicious and the atmosphere was cozy until a certain man arrived and started arguing . . . a plague at the dinner table."

The following day, Erich approached Klara in the restaurant and said, "May I introduce myself? I'm Erich Buchmann."

"My name is Kläre [KLAY-reh] Füting," replied Klara coyly. She thought that Kläre sounded more French, more sophisticated. Erich was smitten. He would call her Kläre from then on, although officially she was Klara. She was pretty, with a joyful smile, stylishly short and curled brunette hair, and a good figure.

Reading this, I realized that my mother was the typical "New Woman" of the twenties, who had changed from long skirts to flapper-style short dresses, cut her long hair into a short bob, and was asserting herself with a good job and with firmly expressed opinions.

"Would you like to go for a walk in the snow on Saturday?" Erich proposed. "We can go to the *Grafenberg* [a nearby mountain]. I may also be able to borrow my landlady's sled."

Klara agreed to go.

Why not? she thought . . . *Let's see how it goes.*

Saturday was sunny and the wintry landscape sparkled. The two enjoyed walking in the fresh air, although Klara noticed that the promised sled had not materialized. No matter—there was much to talk about, and the time flew. With red cheeks, they entered the Café Kürten and ordered *Kaffee mit Schlag und Kuchen* (coffee with whipped cream and cake). Now their talk became more specific about each other.

"So . . . How long have you been at Rheinmetall?" asked Klara.

"Since October first. I just got my PhD in physics."

"Oh, really? Where did you study?"

"I had two semesters at the university in Bonn, one in Vienna, one in Munich, and four in Kiel. I've been fortunate." Erich continued, "I've met some of the greats in physics, even Niels Bohr and Werner Heisenberg."

Klara observed Erich. He appeared strong and self-assured. She liked his sandy hair and blue eyes. "Was it difficult, to study physics?" she asked.

"Well, it wasn't easy. But I'm excited about all the tremendous advances being made in physics all the time now. And we've got so many great challenges still ahead. Future research will be interesting." Erich paused to pass the sugar to Klara and then asked, "Do you like your work at the company?"

"I do like it. It can be a challenge to keep up with all my languages, but I'm up to it. So tell me more about your studies."

"My majors were physics and mathematics and my minor was chemistry. You know, Kläre, there were only six to ten students in many of my classes and most of them planned to be teachers. But because I intend to do research my professors gave me extra time."

"That must have given you a boost."

"Oh yes, naturally. I always met with my professors at the beginning of each term to plan my studies, what classes to take and what labs. But after that it was up to me. We didn't have any exams until the semester was over, so we had to be self-motivated for months. A lot of students find that quite difficult—to be completely on their own during their studies until exam time, but, you know, I enjoyed that."

Klara nodded, listening attentively. Both took a sip of coffee and a bite of cake, and Erich continued. "I studied hard, because I knew that if I kept up a high average, tuition was free. That was very important to me because there are thirteen children in my family and they are all going to go to a university."

"Thirteen children?" Klara was stunned. "How can your family afford this?"

"Well," Erich laughed, "the older children have to commit to help the younger ones. You know, I'm from a village called Voerde, in the Rhineland, and I started out in a one-room schoolhouse."

"Well, I guess you did very well. I started out in a convent school in Werne. College was not affordable for my mother, but I had extra training in languages and in typing and stenography."

"So, you've come a long way, too, Kläre."

"Yes, I think so. And what are your plans now?" Klara asked, slowly sipping the wonderful, strong coffee topped with whipped cream. Having survived the war in their teens, and the hard times afterward, Klara and Erich were happy to have an occasional indulgence.

After munching his *Sachertorte* (a rich chocolate cake with apricot flavoring), Erich answered thoughtfully, "I'm thinking of applying to a research lab in Kiel. It would be a civil service job, under the auspices of the navy. They're studying how ships react to underwater vibrations. It's a government job, with security and advancements and good salary and benefits."

"Well, I don't understand anything about physics," said Klara lightly. "I'm more interested in languages and the arts. Have you read that new novel, *Im Westen nichts Neues* [*All Quiet on the Western Front*], by Erich Maria Remarque?"

"Yes, as a matter of fact I have. I think it's a gripping book, very realistic. Tells the horrible truth about what war in the trenches is really like. I just finished it."

"I did, too!" Klara eagerly responded. "It just confirms my opinion that war is terrible and futile. That book makes it so dreadfully vivid and obvious. I hope we'll never have another war again."

Erich nodded, paid the check, and turned to Klara. "Say, how about another outing next Saturday? I'll bring that sled." Klara agreed.

On the following weekend the two young people met again. As they walked along, arm in arm, Klara asked, "Where's the sled?"

"Oh, my landlady lent it to someone else."

The two enjoyed a long, brisk walk on foot and then visited the café again with red cheeks to sit down over coffee and cake and talk and talk.

"So, Kläre, how long have you been working here in Düsseldorf?" asked Erich.

"I've been here almost three years. I love Düsseldorf, don't you?"

"Yes. It's a beautiful and cosmopolitan city. And meeting you has made it even better for me. Tell me, where did you work before?"

Klara answered, "My first good job was as a stenographer and typist in German, French, English, and occasionally even some Spanish. That was from 1925 to 1926 in Duisburg. Then I wanted to spend some time honing my French language skills, so I got a job with Transimex in Antwerp, Belgium, for six months and with Forceville for another eight months. I had to speak French almost all the time. And that was hard at first, believe me. I didn't know anybody either, so I was a little lonely. But I met the challenge! And it was exciting to improve so quickly. Then after I'd done a lot of translating of business letters and documents, they let me write correspondence on my own, both technical and sales. I got a big raise, too. I was proud of that, but I was glad when a job opened up here in Düsseldorf. I have family here."

"So what exactly was that job here?"

"I worked at Aloverzee; that's a part of Krupp Ironworks. I was there for about fifteen months and then switched to Rheinmetall here."

"And here you do what exactly?"

"I do correspondence in German, French, and English. It can be trying, but I've done quite well."

"I certainly admire your language skills, Kläre."

"Thank you. I'm happy working here."

Erich said, "I am, too, but for me it's not enough of a challenge and the advancement prospects are not great."

Klara wrote in her diary that night: "We have a good time, but we also argue a lot. We have different opinions on many topics, like politics and religion. I'm more liberal than Erich is."

Nevertheless, the two continued to see each other frequently, sometimes enjoying each other's company and sometimes arguing. Walking along the beautiful Rhine riverfront promenade one day, Erich said to Klara, "I know you were raised a Catholic, but I don't understand how you can believe that the pope is the one person on earth who best understands the word of God."

Klara didn't like Erich's argumentative tone.

"I'm not a practicing Catholic," she said, "and I don't believe in the ultimate authority of the pope, but I do feel that Catholicism is a warm religion. The cathedrals are beautiful and I like the impressive ancient ritual of the mass. I also think it's easier for many people to send a little prayer to an intermediate who seems more approachable than the awe-inspiring God the Father. It's more comfortable asking St. Christopher for a safe trip when you'll be traveling, or St. Anthony for help when you've lost something. And a woman likes to address Mary in her prayers. It seems that she'd understand women's problems better."

Erich stopped walking, turned to Klara, and said earnestly, "Yes, I can see how you feel about that."

On another occasion, walking along the Rhine promenade again, Erich told Klara, "Let's sit down here. I want to tell you a little about my family's religious background." The two sat down on a bench by the river as Erich went on. "You need to know that I come from a family that's quite religious. We're Protestants, Evangelical Lutherans, and we also belong to a small group that meets every week in someone's house for the *Stunde*. That's an hour of scripture reading and discussion. We feel that we can approach God directly, without the intercession of a pastor or priest or saint. The responsibility to be good Christians is up to us."

Looking up into Erich's eyes, Klara replied, "I consider myself a freethinker, but I can understand and respect what you're saying. I want you to understand and respect my background a little more also. My father was Friedrich Füting, and the whole Füting clan is Protestant. But my mother, Johanna Sieben, was Catholic, and that's why we three sisters were raised Catholic."

This conversation gave both young people much to think about.

The romance stuttered along, with get-togethers of attraction and harmony, interspersed with some serious disagreements. Klara and Erich did not date exclusively. The Carnival on the Rhine Festival was attended by both—but not together. And during the Artists' Ball at the Academy, a costumed young man and a female "Turkish boy" danced by each other, unaware of who they were, as they discovered to their surprise later when they happened to talk about the ball.

As spring arrived in Düsseldorf, Klara decided to invite Erich to meet her aunt and uncle, the older couple with whom she was staying. Klara was very attached to her aunt, "Tante Johanna," and her uncle by marriage, "Onkel Toni" Bochum, who had been her parent substitutes for several years. They had no children, but a lively purebred dachshund was part of their family. Klara's mother had just died recently, of pernicious anemia.

It is sad that only a few years later this became an illness curable by vitamin B12.

I think that mother and daughter had not been very close. Klara never talked about her father or mother and never mentioned hugs or kisses or even praise and encouragement. Her mother had been stressed and bitter after her husband, Klara's father, died young and unexpectedly, leaving her with three little children and not much money. Life insurance was not a common practice at that time. Klara was still a toddler and did not remember her father. The family had to move to the small town of Werne, where her mother could find some work. A brother, Klara's "rich uncle from Köln*" (Cologne), helped the family out. But then another tragedy occurred when Klara, age nine, and her two older sisters developed severe typhoid fever and the eldest died. Klara (my "Mutti" [MOOT-tee]), told us that she remembers the sister (a nursing nun) coming to the house and telling her mother, "This little one won't make it, either." (She was very wrong; Klara lived to be almost ninety!)*

Now, after her mother's death, Klara had only one older sister, Erna, as immediate family.

When the couple arrived at the spacious apartment, Erich immediately made friends with Helga, the dachshund, and therefore also with Tante Johanna and Onkel Toni. They all had a good time together getting acquainted over coffee and pastries, and afterward Klara and Erich took the dog for a walk.

Helga, the dachshund, played cupid as the two young humans enjoyed the budding chestnut trees along the elegant Königsallee, Düsseldorf's main avenue. They did some window-shopping along the boutiques and cafes and afterward walked to the *Hofgarten* (chateau garden) to view the cherry blossoms. Klara said, "I think that Tante Johanna and Onkel Toni liked you." Erich smiled and stole a kiss under the canopy of pink-and-white blossoms, while the dachshund looked on, wagging her tail.

Evening walks along the dark, shimmering Rhine furthered the romance, but arguments kept erupting. Klara especially didn't like the prospect of Erich leaving Düsseldorf in the fall to work in Kiel, since she had become so attached to her lovely city.

"But why move to Kiel?" she pouted. "Düsseldorf is so much more interesting."

Erich pointed out again that his career opportunities were limited here, but quite promising in Kiel.

Early in the summer, the two young people enjoyed a harmonious outing to Kaiserswerth am Rhein, where they took photos of each other, which Klara saved in her diary/photo album. But later in the summer they both went on separate vacations again.

In the fall they had to say goodbye to each other, since Erich was leaving for Kiel, located in the north of Germany on the Baltic Sea. He kept in touch with many letters, however, and Klara answered.

The two confessed that they missed each other and Erich visited at Christmas. They had a good time together with no serious quarrel. Erich broached the idea of getting together permanently.

He was in love with Klara and wanted a wife by his side as he was building his career. Klara still resisted the idea of moving to Kiel. But she was twenty-eight years old and wanted to get married and have children.

"I was not meant to be an old spinster," she wrote in her diary. "I just want to be somebody having a full life. Not like my older sister, Erna, living in the little town of Werne and teaching in a convent school."

Klara was three years older than Erich and that bothered her so much that she never admitted it voluntarily. For the rest of her life, she didn't like the age difference mentioned.

The two discussed having children. Both wanted a family. Klara agreed that if it came to that point she would let the children be raised as Lutherans, although she would reserve the right to her own liberal religious views with a Catholic slant. But then Klara wrote in her diary, "We've had another fight." Stubbornly, they parted again.

Erich celebrated New Year's Eve in Kiel. Klara went to Paris for an interesting week.

Could this love affair survive?

CHAPTER 2

1930: Klara and Erich marry and settle in Kiel.
1931: Visits to Klara's sister in Werne and to Erich's family in Voerde.
Fifteen Buchmann siblings listed.

Erich did not give up. Although he had to devote most of his time and energy to his new job in Kiel, he wrote Klara often. He described his work as a research associate at the Physics and Chemistry Research Station of the Navy in broad outline and told Klara that he missed her. She wrote back, relating what was happening in Düsseldorf.

I'm sorry that I don't have the letters as a resource. My father told me decades later that he had bought a fireproof lockbox to preserve these love letters, but they were destroyed when a bomb fell near our Berlin apartment, causing shrapnel damage, including to the piano, and some fire. When he later opened the box, there were only charred papers inside. I could always hear great sadness in his voice when he told me about this loss. Here is what I imagine he might have written on one occasion to overcome Klara's resistance: "Dear Klara, how are you? I miss you and your company so much. I admire your intellectual curiosity, your independent spirit, and your beautiful legs. I'd like you to give me a little kiss when I see you next."

Klara had still not decided whether to go ahead with future plans for herself and Erich, but she was leaning that way. She thought, "Erich loves me and I like his looks and his company. He's got a good future. I'm falling in love with him, too. I guess I'll have to make that move from Düsseldorf to Kiel. After all, I'm not getting any younger, and I want a full life with marriage and children."

At Eastertime, the two took a three-day holiday in Hannover, and this time they just had a good time together without ever quarreling. And shortly thereafter, Erich proposed and Klara accepted!

The engaged couple spent August vacationing together in various parts of Germany. Erich had bought a motorcycle and Klara sat behind him, elegant in a cloche hat, suede jacket, knee-length skirt, hose, and moderate heels. *I have a lovely photo of them.* "This is a very good motorcycle," she yelled as they rode along. "Such fun!" She trusted Erich completely and enjoyed holding on to him, and that gave her a secure feeling for the upcoming marriage.

The couple visited Klara's birthplace, Kupfermühle, in Denmark, not far from the extreme north of Germany. This town has at various times been German or Danish. They took pictures of her childhood home, a beautiful mansion with park-like grounds. According to the comment on one photo, they even met the old gardener, who remembered Klara taking her first steps.

What a surprise it was for me to find these pictures! My Mutti had never talked about these early years of her life. Her family must have been very well off until her father died young, and then there was a great change in their circumstances. Klara herself probably didn't remember much of these early years.

Next the couple traveled on to Hamburg, and then down to the beautiful Lüneburger Heide, purple with heather. Finally, they hiked on the Brocken Mountain trails.

At the end of the month, the two were married in a civil ceremony. *I have the official marriage certificate and translated it. It reads in part:*

> ". . . Düsseldorf North. On the thirtieth of August, nineteen hundred thirty. The following persons appeared before the magistrate for the Purpose of Marriage: The research associate Erich Hermann Buchmann, PhD, born June 18, 1904, in Voerde, lower Rhineland, as per birth certificate, now residing in Kiel; and Hilde Klara Karoline Füting, corresponding secretary, born November 7, 1901, in Kupfermühle, now in Denmark, as per birth

certificate, now residing in Düsseldorf. Witnesses: Corresponding secretary Wilhelmina Koors, age twenty-four . . . and Engineer Richard Braun, age twenty-nine . . . Marriage certified . . ."

Erich now returned to Kiel, and Klara prepared to leave Düsseldorf at the end of the year. Erich wrote, "Klara, you're going to like living in Kiel! True, it's not as large and cosmopolitan as Düsseldorf, but it has theaters, music, parks, and lovely residential areas. And here's a plus: the beach is only thirty minutes away. I have found us an apartment facing an avenue that has a green park space between the lanes, perfect for daily walks. The address is Habsburgerring 2. [The name later changed to Weddigenring.] And there is a courtyard in the back. We'll have two bedrooms, a dining room, a living room, and a kitchen with a balcony. It's all *parterre* [on the first floor]. You'll love it."

On December 24, Christmas Eve, 1930, the couple celebrated with a church wedding in Düsseldorf—a small ceremony in an Evangelical Lutheran church, attended by nearby family and friends.

I still have the Bible my parents received on this occasion, inscribed by Pastor W. v. Langenhohe, VDM, and looking at it I imagine my parents as newlyweds. The wedding scripture was Galatians 6:2. ("Bear one another's burdens, and so fulfill the laws of Christ.")

Erich returned to Kiel, and Klara took a few days to say her goodbyes to Tante Johanna, Onkel Toni, coworkers and friends, her beloved Rhine riverfront, and Düsseldorf. Her colleagues gave her a goodbye toast and roast, including a "final report card." *I found it among my source papers and translated it as follows:*

> Miss Füting has been thoroughly troublesome for over two and a half years. Although she was a loyal employee for her bosses, she was a stubborn-headed Westphalian colleague for us. She only shared her chocolate when she'd had enough and only got coffee for us when she needed some herself for a hangover. And that whistling! Morning, noon, and night! And she opened the windows when it was zero degrees outside. The high phone bills were all her fault, too—always making dates for coffee with all her girlfriends. Now she's leaving, thank goodness, and will quit bothering us, and instead pester her husband. Nevertheless, we're afraid we'll miss her!
>
> All good wishes for the future!
> The firm
> Signed: Ebner, Steel Sales

Klara graciously donated the last of her bittersweet chocolate plus an apple to her friends. Chocolate and apples had been her pick-me-ups during long afternoon translations. "Besides being with Erich, there's another plus of marriage," she told her coworkers. "Now I can work when I feel like it, with no deadlines."

Klara moved to Kiel and the newlyweds started to feather their nest. Klara had never run a household before and threw herself into all the new duties with joy and enthusiasm. While Erich worked,

Klara explored the neighborhood. She found a baker nearby and arranged to have *Brötchen* (breakfast hard rolls) delivered fresh every morning. Mmmm—that wonderful aroma! She also made sure that milk and butter were delivered. The glass bottles of milk showed a two-inch level of cream at the top, which Klara carefully decanted to use with coffee. The kitchen's icebox was tiny. In the winter, milk and cream were often stored on the cool windowsill. Klara, like every housewife, had to plan a shopping trip daily. That wasn't bad; it got her out of the house and provided plenty of exercise, since all these errands were done on foot. The butcher and greengrocer were nearby. Klara learned to cook a bit and she also met several neighbors and began to make new friends.

In her leisure time, she read. She enjoyed Thomas Mann's novels, for which the author had won the Nobel Prize for literature in 1929. She read *Die Buddenbrooks,* a grand family saga, and *Der Zauberberg* (*The Magic Mountain*). *I still have these books, in German, with Klara's notes in the margins.* "I can't put this book down," she told Erich over their evening sandwiches one day, referring to *Der Zauberberg.* "It's such a bittersweet story of young persons with consumption—you know—tuberculosis. They're confined to a mountaintop sanatorium for a long time in the hope that fresh air, good food, and rest might help cure their lungs. Mann describes so well their fear of death when they suddenly cough up blood, their hope for health when they gain a pound or two, and their desperate partying to enjoy what life is left to them. I'm so deeply touched by this novel. It's sad when young people are infected with such a dreadful wasting disease and have to spend months and years away from their families and school and career without certainty of the outcome." *As I read my mother's notes, I am struck by the similarity of the situation with that of AIDS in the twentieth century. Little could my mother know that one day she would have a daughter who would become a physician and often treat patients with tuberculosis and sometimes also AIDS. And she would have a pediatrician son-in-law, who often treated children with AIDS.*

Erich enjoyed being married to Klara, who kept him up to date on the latest cultural and fashion events. Klara, in turn, loved being a married woman and having a loyal and loving husband, who was making steady progress in his career.

Klara began to write articles for a local newspaper and for a women's magazine. Soon she had a weekly column on exploring neighboring nature and historic spots, which she and Erich visited most weekends on their motorcycle or on bicycles.

Both Erich and Klara enjoyed furnishing their new home. They bought two walnut beds and pushed them together to make a double-sized one. Klara found a down-filled comforter in a pretty shade of dusky rose. A large armoire held clothing. (*There were no closets.*) On the mirror above the dresser Klara taped a few religious cards—angels and nativity scenes from famous paintings.

The couple bought their dining room furniture and also two simple beds and a dresser for the guest bedroom. For the living room, Klara picked a suite of two upholstered chairs and a sofa in her favorite shade of dusky rose. *I remember that they felt very firm to sit on. Perhaps their sturdiness helped them survive throughout Klara's and Erich's life, a war, and emigration to America.* Erich also got a card table and chairs for frequent card games of *Skat* with friends. The young couple hung reproductions of old masters. A self-portrait of *Rembrandt as a Young Man* was on prominent display over the sofa. (*This rather gloomy painting also later made its way to the United States, where it hung in the living room over the sofa and frightened Klara's and Erich's little granddaughter, Cindy.*) Erich and Klara found a truly magnificent, huge, glass-front mahogany bookcase, elegantly bowed at the top. It filled quickly, since both Klara and Erich were ravenous readers. (*I remember my Papa lifting me on his shoulders and then setting me atop the bookcase. I loved sitting up so high, with a slight twinge of anxiety and a great feeling of exhilaration at being taller than anyone.*)

On the twelfth day of March, 1930, the newspapers headlined Mahatma Gandhi's 240-mile march, his act of civil disobedience that marked the beginning of Indian independence and of the disintegration of the British empire.

"Oh, I really admire that man," Klara told Erich at breakfast, over coffee and a roll with butter and *Marmelade* (jam). "How brave of him to collect so many supporters and walk so far—unarmed—

while the British have troops and tanks." (*As I read these notes, the comparison with Martin Luther King's civil rights marches in the 1960s immediately came to mind.*)

"The British also have trained a large Indian army to support them," answered Erich. "I'm afraid for Gandhi and his supporters. But really, it's a great and revolutionary idea: Passive resistance used against an occupying force that is the strongest in the entire world! A non-bloody revolution in the cause of liberty! I wish all changes could be accomplished without war."

Klara said, "Having lived through 'the war to end all wars' [World War I] in my teens has colored my opinion of all wars. It was terrible. So many men lost, so many women without a possible partner for their lives; just look at my older sister, Erna. So many children fatherless. And Erich, can you believe this? I remember my mother giving her few gold items, a watch and some coins, for the cause and the Kaiser." (*Reading this reminds me of my college world history classes. Max Weber, the eminent social historian, described so well that there was still a strong personal connection between subjects and ruler at the time of World War I in Germany, a traditional form of* Herrschaft *[rule], which to some degree still persists in England. The British monarchy survived after World War I, while most European ones were toppled. The king, the German* Kaiser, *and the Russian* tsar *were all first cousins!*)

Klara: "After the war, we were all wiped out. And for what?"

Erich: "Well, perhaps there are some just wars, but in general I must agree with you."

Klara: "I'm not a political person and I'm strictly a pacifist. If I were a man, I would be a conscientious objector."

And so the days passed. In 1931, the couple made many short and long trips throughout Germany. They thoroughly enjoyed traveling together. They took their usual four-week vacation in August. Germans had received generous social benefits, including long vacations, social security, and national disability and health insurance since the time of Bismark in the late 1800s. The couple visited Klara's sister, Erna, in Werne, where the sisters grew up. Erna was not married—one of the victims of the lack of men after the war, as Klara had mentioned to Erich. She seemed content, however, with her life as a teacher in the little town. She was reserved and serious, very different from her strong-willed, spirited younger sister. Klara showed Erich her old home, to which the family had moved from Kupfermühle, after Klara's father died at a young age. She also showed him her school and the lovely landscape in which she used to roam. Together they all visited her mother's grave and took some hikes in the mountains.

After Werne, the two planned their visit to the village of Voerde, where Erich had grown up. He got out a map and showed her the location, close to the lower Rhine River. "You see," he pointed out, "on the left of the Rhine, that's west, is Holland. The French came through there and crossed the Rhine after the war in 1918, because they wanted to assure themselves that the Ruhr area would give up a large percentage of its steel to France. That occupation was actually illegal after the Treaty of Versailles and made us very angry, since we already had an unbearable burden of so-called reparations. It was also unfair in the first place to blame Germany for this war and I've read, even in English papers, that many historians actually agree about that. I saw these French troops, by the way, when I was in school."

"That must have made a big impression on you. You still sound mad."

"You're not kidding."

Klara said, *"Na ja* [NAH yah].*"* (*It roughly corresponds to "Oh well." I can still hear Mutti and Papa using this common expression.*)

"Na ja, now you'll have to bring me up to date on all your brothers and sisters. You have so many that I'm quite confused about their order."

"Ja [Yah], fine," replied Erich. "Remember, my mother is called *Mutter* [MOOT-tah] by us and my father is called *Vater* [FAAH-tah]. He's the manager of the dairy in Voerde. Mutter had fifteen children, but two died in infancy. Are you sure you really want to know all their names and birth order? I don't think you can remember that right now."

"Au contraire, mon ami! [On the contrary, my dear! *Klara often used French expressions in her speech. It was considered fashionable at that time.*] Listen, Erich, I'm in the family now. Of course I want to know. And

I want to meet as many as possible as soon as possible. I'm going to get a sheet of paper and list all you siblings with a few dates and details." Klara got up to get a pad of paper from the desk and a fountain pen, seated herself at the dining table, and looked at Erich expectantly.

"Okay then, here goes. I'll take all my brothers and sisters in order of birth:

"1. 1895: Helena. She only lived two months."

"Oh no, how terrible!" interjected Klara. "She was Mutter's first child. It must have been devastating."

Erich nodded and continued: "I'm not sure why the baby died, but they told us she had 'cramps,' but not intestinal cramps.

"2. 1896: Frieda. She's married to Erich Rickmann and they have a daughter, Elle. They live in Voerde and you'll meet them.

"3. 1898: Else. She's a schoolteacher and she's been a mother's helper for all of us younger children as we came along. Mutter has always had two maids, but with all the employees at Vater's dairy eating their meals at the house, plus all the children to look after, plus the garden and chickens, she needed even more help. We call Else *das Familienauge* [the eye of the family]. She was a little bit despotic, but nevertheless loving when I was little, and now she's purely supportive of all of us younger children. She never married and really devoted her life to us. You'll meet her.

"4. 1900: Hedwig. Hers is a sad story. She used to race around as a girl, but when she was fourteen she developed polio. And after that she's been in a wheelchair."

"Oh, how horrible!" cried Klara. "That's just too much. Such a tragedy."

"Hedwig works in Vater's office. He's the local dairy manager, as you know, and she keeps the books. Hedwig has a lively imagination. She can keep us spellbound with her stories, and we never know what's fiction or fact. When she was younger she had a whole group of imaginary children. She had them sitting on chairs and addressed them all by name: Annemarie, Philippine, and so on." Erich started laughing and Klara joined in.

"5. 1901: Marta. She only lived ten months and also died of cramps."

By now, Klara was silent about the sad event and just took notes.

"6. 1903: Hans (Johannes), the first boy. He's married to someone also called Else and they have a son, Heinz. They run the restaurant and hotel at the railroad station in Voerde. But now Hans is beginning to take over the management of the dairy, since Vater is sixty-five. You'll meet all of these relatives. Don't get overwhelmed." (*I remember playing with Heinz in the backyard in Voerde.*)

"7. 1904: Erich. That's me. I hope you know a lot about me already," he laughed. Klara gave him a hug.

"8. 1906: Ewald. He followed in my footsteps and is studying physics. He's also good in ancient languages. Can you believe that he gave his high school valedictorian address in Greek?"

Klara laughed, "I doubt many people understood him."

Ewald became a director of the large firm Siemens.

"9. 1907: Ernst. He's also studying physics. I really started something, didn't I?

He's so relaxed that once, during the horrendously difficult *Abitur* exam (*which qualifies students to go to the university*), he rewrote a topic subject the teacher had put on the blackboard in such a funny way that he made the whole class laugh."

Ernst also became a director of Siemens. He was interested not only in physics, but also in philosophy and poetry. My college boyfriend, Rod Boes, and I had a lively correspondence with Ernst for a while.

"10. 1909: Magdalene. She's planning to be a teacher."

Her husband was killed in World War II. She went on to become a teacher, but never married.

"11. 1911: Kurt. He's in college, studying physics and chemistry also. That's the fourth boy to go into physics. We'll probably have to help him get through his studies. He may have to stay with us in Kiel, if he studies there."

Klara said, "That'll be fine, I'm sure."

Kurt later also worked at Siemens. He and his wife, Maria Tenzer, became good friends with me and my second husband, Don Norton, when we visited Munich, Germany, in 1994 and when she visited us in Atlanta, Georgia, in 1995.

"12. 1912: Hermann. He's studying in Bonn and being supported by Else. He's the comic of the family, always telling jokes. I think he wants to teach."

He became a gymnasium principal.

"13. 1914: Werner. Very talented. Still in high school."

He was tragically killed in World War II.

"14. 1916: Ruth. She was born during the war [World War I]. She's into sports and a very pretty, blond, blue-eyed teenager."

She married Heinrich Feldkamp and had two children, Uwe and Swantje. I met them in Voerde during World War II in 1942 when they were toddlers and then again at a family reunion in Germany in 2011. They were instantly familiar and very warm and loving to me and my son, Eddy, and ten-year-old grandson, Lucas.

"15. 1919: Helmut. He's the youngest. Mutter was forty years old when he was born, the last of fifteen children, starting with Helena when Mutter was twenty."

Helmut was reported missing in action early in World War II on a naval reconnaissance flight over the English Channel. He was only twenty.

Klara sat back and looked at Erich. "It's almost unbelievable. But I've got everything written down on this sheet."

Erich laughed, "Well, just be sure to have this cheat sheet with you when we get to Voerde and you'll really impress everyone. I hope our big family isn't too much to take."

Klara shook her head. "No, Erich, I find it wonderful and enriching. My family is so small now. I really only have contact with my sister occasionally, and with Tante Johanna and Onkel Toni in Düsseldorf. I'm looking forward to meeting your family."

In truth, Klara was very, very worried about encountering this large family. It was so important to her to make a good impression. She was concerned about her looks, her clothes, her religious outlook, her lack of a university education. She wanted to put her best foot forward, make contact, and have a good, close relationship, especially with Erich's father and mother.

Did she succeed?

CHAPTER 3

1931: Visiting Erich's family in Voerde.
Vater and Mutter Buchmann's histories.

Klara and Erich took the train to Voerde. At the station they were met by Hans with a horse and buggy. It was a sunny day and the ride along Frankfurter Strasse was bucolic and peaceful. Black-and-white cows were grazing in the fields. "These are Holsteins," Erich told Klara. "They produce lots of very rich milk with a 3.6 percent fat content. The farmers collect the milk and put it out in those large metal cans you see over there by the street, and then from there the milk is taken to the dairy." Klara nodded, looking left and right.

She turned to Hans. "Thanks for picking us up. I understand you're taking over the dairy and mill management so that Vater can retire."

Hans was a sturdy man, not intellectual by nature, but able and hardworking. "Yes, you're right about that. It's so nice to meet you. You're very welcome here."

They arrived at Frankfurter Strasse 2a and Klara was amazed and impressed by the large and attractive house. (*I own an aerial photo of it, which I have framed and hung with photos and paintings of other houses I've lived in.*) Erich and Klara were welcomed at the door by Mutter, Friederike Buchmann. Dressed in black with a large apron, she exclaimed, "Well there you are!" with a big smile. Her waist had thickened after so many children, but she was still slim and lively. She embraced Klara and Erich and said, "Come in and let's go upstairs." She led Klara and Erich to a second-floor bedroom fronting the street. "Make yourselves at home. Erich will show you around, Klara. Dinner is at noon." This would be the main meal of the day, as usual in Germany.

At the large dinner table, Erich introduced his new bride to the assembled family and others. Klara charmed them all and Erich was proud of her. However, that night Klara wrote in her diary: "I almost fainted when we sat down to dinner. Twenty-four people around the table! Mutter and Vater presiding, Erich and I, eleven other family members, two maids, an elderly lady who lost her home and has been taken in as a seamstress, and six employees from the dairy."

Vater, Johann Buchmann, led off the meal with a scripture reading. Then everyone sang a hymn, after which plates of hot milk soup with bread croutons were handed around. The next course featured *Bratkartoffeln* (home fries). Meat was chicken from the coop in back of the house. Fresh vegetables from the garden rounded out the delicious and healthful meal. No dessert was served. There was plenty of milk and buttermilk to drink.

I have tried to duplicate those wonderful Bratkartoffeln all my life. No luck. The secret must have been in the type of fat used, perhaps goose grease from their own free-range geese.

Vigorous discussions flew back and forth during the entire dinner, covering topics from philosophy, politics, and the latest scientific achievements, to the weather, the state of the dairy, and crops on neighboring farms. The maids and hands didn't say much, but the family members obviously enjoyed a spirited exchange of opinions and would have continued for a long time if Mutter had not stopped the talk by saying, "All right, that's all for now. The maids have to clean up and rest a bit." After dinner, there was another prayer, and then everyone returned to work.

Klara followed Vater after the meal and sat down with him in the large living room, furnished Victorian-style with mahogany tables, upholstered sofas and chairs, and heavy drapes at the windows. Vater settled himself comfortably on a chair, with the sun shining in from a window behind him, and Klara sat down on a sofa. She asked him how he got into dairy management.

The following dialog is imagined by me, since I don't remember my grandfather. I was told that he spoke in a slow and deliberate way, and I know that he was very religious from what my Papa (Erich) wrote about him. I also have a book about Brünen, Vater's birthplace, which gives a very detailed history of names, farms, costs of buying and selling land and items, and politics.

Vater said, "*Na ja*, you see, I was raised on a large farm in Brünen. That's a village near Wesel, about a half hour from here. The village Brünen goes back all the way to the year 809. Our family farm there is called Krebbinghof. That name and the name Buchmann—sometimes it's also spelled Buschmann—and my mother's maiden name, Tinnefeld, can be found in the Brünen records by the early 1300s. So you see I have deep roots there."

Klara nodded her head, feeling quite impressed by this long history back to medieval times.

"Things don't change quickly in Brünen," Vater continued. "People are very set in their ways. And they watch each other and talk about each other. Just as an example, let me tell you that when we bought that sofa you're sitting on, my family in Brünen voiced their disapproval. They thought it was an unnecessary luxury." Vater smiled, leaned forward, and went on. "I knew early on in my life that I couldn't stay and make it on our farm. I have ten sisters and brothers and realized I had to set off to do something on my own."

He leaned back in his easy chair at this time of after-dinner repose, which was still new to him, and continued, "When I was twenty, I was drafted into the Prussian army and served two years at Metz. That's the first time I saw anything away from our village. At home we were very traditional, but in the army I saw a wider world. I learned to enjoy sports and I also began to realize the value of a good education. That's why I want all of our children to go to a university."

Klara mentioned how impressed she had been when Erich had told her about these ambitious plans.

Vater was pleased to hear that. "After my discharge" he said, "I worked for a few years as foreman on a large farm, 'Schultz Buhnert,' in Brünen and that's where I met my future wife, Friederike Weier. She was also working there and we hit it off right away. We were married on November 9, 1894."

"How old was Friederike at that time?"

"She was nineteen and I was twenty-five. We had our first two children there in Brünen. I thought I might lease and then buy us a farm somewhere else perhaps, but the owner of the Schultz Buhnert farm sat down with me one day and said, 'You're an excellent worker, but you won't be able to afford a large enough farm for a long time, despite all your hard work. How about learning how to run a business, like a dairy, and managing that? That would give you better prospects for the future. I'll help you.'"

Vater paused, silently reminiscing, and then proceeded with his story. "So I took his advice and went to school in Hameln to learn managerial skills, especially how to direct a successful dairy. I'm sure you've heard of Hameln, the town famous for the Pied Piper?"

"Oh, yes," Klara perked up. "The Pied Piper was hired to play his pipe—a kind of flute I guess, or a penny whistle—and lure the rats out of town, wasn't he? He must have worn 'pied' clothes, made of colorful patches. And he was successful in his boasting that he could get the rats to follow him. Then the town officials didn't pay him what they had promised. And the Pied Piper took revenge by luring the town's children out by playing his pipe. They were never seen again."

"Yes, that's the story. Well, that's where I studied. And then I became assistant manager of a dairy in the Brünen area. I did the bookkeeping, buying, and selling, and supervised all the steps in milk processing. You know—cream, butter, buttermilk, skim milk, and cottage cheese."

Vater was flattered by Klara's intense attention and interest and continued his history. "When I was thirty-two, I was offered the job as manager of the Voerde dairy. I was excited about that and moved my family to Voerde. We lived in the house behind the dairy at first. That's called 'the old house' now, and that's where Hans and Else now live with little Heinz. Then we built this 'new house' here. It's been good for us, by the grace of God."

The conversation brought Klara and Vater closer.

Klara continued, "I was surprised to see how big and beautiful this house is—three stories, so many bedrooms! I especially love that huge bathroom downstairs with the great yellow, tiled tub."

Vater: "*Na ja*, we have a large family and need a lot of room."

Klara: "I have the impression, Vater, that you're a very devout man."

Vater: "You're right, Klara, I'm God fearing and I believe in the scriptures and in prayer. But I'm also open minded. If someone's a good person, that's what counts for me."

Klara was so happy that she had started on the right foot with Vater. She wanted to know more about his family, but decided to save that for another day.

One day Erich took Klara to the dairy and showed her the steel vats where milk was churned for butter and buttermilk. Other vats produced cottage cheese and *Quark* (a delicious kind of farmer cheese). Klara got to see the mill, too, where rows of sacks full of grain were stacked high. She liked the warm smell of grain and straw and suddenly called out, "Erich, come here and look!" Delightedly she showed him a mother cat with her kittens in a corner. Erich and Klara bent down to stroke the kittens' soft fur.

On the next day Erich took Klara to meet some of the neighboring farmers. They talked about life in the country, about Erich when he was a little boy, about the war of 1914 to 1918, and about the difficult times at present. They were all happy to be living on farms, where they could always be sure to have enough to eat; however, finding jobs to earn extra money was very difficult. Klara and Erich explored the farmyards, swarming with chickens and a few roosters scratching in the dirt. They saw barns filled with hay and straw in the lofts and cattle and horse stalls below. Barn cats and yard dogs snoozed in the sun. Pigs snuffled in pens in the back. Apple trees were heavily laden with fruit. Flies and bees buzzed everywhere.

One afternoon the couple borrowed the horse and buggy to ride through the lovely landscape. "What's growing in those fields?" asked Klara. Erich smiled. Klara was a city girl and didn't know the different grains. "Over there on the right, that's rye. It's tall and looks sort of grayish green. But here on the left, that's wheat. It's yellow and thicker. And that over there, with the bigger grains, is barley." They drove on and watched a hay baler go through a pasture, leaving little packets of hay. Klara recognized the corn fields, and she also recognized the Holstein cows. Erich was glad to see his sophisticated wife enjoying the country.

The next morning Klara caught Mutter in the kitchen. "Can I help?"

"*Na ja*," said Mutter, "how about hulling these peas?"

Klara was still amazed at the enormous quantities of food necessary for this large group of people as she stared at the bottomless bowl of peas to be shelled. Mutter sat down at the table next to Klara and helped one of the maids peel potatoes. Potatoes were included in every noon meal.

"Well, what do you think of Voerde?" Mutter asked.

Klara answered honestly, "I'm really impressed by this beautiful village. Your family and neighbors are very friendly. It's not like in a large city."

Mutter agreed. "Yes, we all know each other well and help out where needed. Everyone works hard, but we have always had enough food, even during the war, thank God, and we've managed to save adequate money to give all the children a higher education. And that's been our primary mission in life."

"How did you ever learn to cook for so many people every day?"

"Oh, you know, I just gradually got used to it," Mutter answered. "You start with a few people, then you add children, then some more employees and maids, then more children . . . and so it goes."

"But how do you take care of so many children? How do you get them into clothes and shoes? How do you supervise their homework and discuss their problems and joys?"

Mutter answered calmly, "Again, you just start with one and gradually learn to take care of more. Don't forget, the older children help take care of the younger ones. And I never supervised their homework; I always felt that was their own business." She smiled. "And it worked, didn't it? To help them in their troubles I always know a Bible verse."

"How many brothers and sisters do you yourself have?" asked Klara as she shelled busily, the little, firm green peas clinking into another bowl and the shells going into a pail at her feet to be fed to the neighbor's pigs later. She found it quite relaxing to keep up a steady pace with her hands.

"I had an older sister and two older brothers," Mutter explained. "We had a small farm and so I left at sixteen to work on a very large farm in Brünen. I sort of helped with everything in the house; that's partly how I learned to manage a large household. It also helped me to be aware of what maids and hands are asked to do, what you can expect from them, and how you have to treat them well.

"I met Johann on that farm; he was the foreman and assistant manager. I liked him because he was honest and hardworking and sincere. I could admire that. I liked his looks, too, dark and interesting, compared to my own family's blond appearance. We fell in love and then we married three years later. We stayed on at that farm a few years more."

Klara asked, "Didn't you have your first babies there?"

"Yes. You know, Klara, when my first baby was born there I was so happy; and then when she died, just three days later, I wanted to die, too. But we're hardened." She paused. "Living on a farm, we see life and death often and know we must keep going. And I have a strong faith in God; that helped me to cope. And, of course, then I had another baby and everything was all right."

"I'm looking forward to having children, too," said Klara. She was getting drowsy. The sun was shining into the open, unscreened kitchen windows; flies were buzzing and some of them got caught on the amber flypapers hanging from the ceiling; the dog outside, lying in front of his doghouse, gave a brief bark in his sleep; a sheep in the backyard added a "baa" . . . "Country life agrees with me."

The Voerde experience was powerful for Klara, and she ruminated about it on the return trip to Kiel. "I've learned so much about your family," she said to Erich on the train. "I've seen what it's like in a big family. And I've really enjoyed the country life."

That made Erich happy.

CHAPTER 4

6/30/1932: Brigitte's birth.
Baby care of that period.
Information about Klara's father.

Back in Kiel, Erich said, "Klara, what do you say? Shouldn't we start seriously thinking about having a baby?"

"*Na ja,* I've thought so, too." Klara was also aware that she would turn thirty in November of this year 1931, and that was considered quite old for a first-time mother. And so the two agreed.

The next section of family history is not based on any oral or written information I obtained from my parents, but rather on impressions I gleaned from observing them and on information available about that time. I did, after all, spend the summer after my first year of medical school in 1954 at my boring, but much-appreciated, job as the lone occupant of an office of the Social Hygiene Society in Washington, DC, with little to do but answer the phone occasionally and read the huge collection of books about sexual practices worldwide. I also learned, and later wrote a term paper, about efforts of birth control throughout history. Continuing with the family story . . .

Up to this time, the couple had practiced birth control without explicitly discussing it. During their engagement, Erich used the withdrawal method. Condoms were known, but most young men learned about them from older brothers or friends as a method of prophylaxis in regard to sexually transmitted diseases. Men usually didn't associate condom use with their fiancées or wives. After marriage, the responsibility customarily shifted to the wife. What could she use? Abstinence was unthinkable for a young, healthy couple in love with each other. The method Klara had heard and read about was douching. This meant that after sex, she immediately jumped up and hurried into the bathroom. She took a large, red rubber bag, looking much like a hot-water bottle except for a long tube at the end, filled it with warm water, added a dash of vinegar, and hung it from a hook in the ceiling over the bathtub. Then she reclined in the dry tub, inserted the end of the tube into her vagina, opened the clamp, and flushed out all secretions. Goodbye, sperm, she hoped.

Being able to stop birth control was nice for both partners. Now Erich didn't have to withdraw prematurely and Klara didn't have to rush into the bathroom immediately. Both could enjoy their intimacy more. Klara liked the closeness and cuddling, but she felt Erich's penis more as an intrusion than a welcome visitor and rarely experienced orgasm. Neither, probably, did her close friends with whom she could occasionally discuss this.

At Christmastime 1931, Klara visited the family doctor because she'd missed several periods and felt queasy in the mornings. "Yes," Dr. Wiesemann confirmed, "you're two and a half months pregnant and everything looks fine. Get a little more rest and eat well and I'll schedule regular follow-ups."

It was a joyous time for Klara and Erich, as they prepared a bassinet, bought glass baby bottles and rubber nipples, selected baby outfits, and notified friends and relatives. Early in the new year, they felt the baby moving and called it *Punkel*, a made-up nonsense word.

Klara took good care of herself and walked in the park every day. One evening in February 1932, she was upset as she reported to Erich, "*Ach, Erich* [Oh, Erich. *This became a lifelong standard expression for her. The "Ach" is pronounced as for the composer, Bach, with a soft throat "ch," as if trying to blow out bit of pollen*], you know I took a walk this morning and on every park bench I saw some young men loitering. I couldn't even sit down somewhere to rest. *Na ja,* I do feel sorry for them not having a job. *Arbeitslosigkeit* [unemployment]—that's the major problem these days. But as I was strolling along, I overheard one of the guys say to another, 'Who'd want to have a baby in these times?'"

Erich hugged Klara and said, "Well, we do!" At the evening meal, Klara made sure to drink a glass of *Hefe Weissbier,* a beer brewed with yeast, which was recommended for its relaxing value and for its vitamin-B content. Erich made sure he got the same benefits also!

On June 29, 1932, as Klara and Erich were attending a friend's 4:00-p.m. wedding in the university chapel, Klara's water broke and labor began. She was surprised because the due date was still two weeks away. Quickly the couple returned home and called the *Hebamme* (midwife; literally, lifting nurse).

"Ow," cried Klara, "it hurts much more than I thought it would!" Sister Marie, a nurse-midwife belonging to a religious order, arrived at 8:00 p.m. She put a protective rubber sheet on the bed, covered by soft flannel, and asked Klara to lie down. She checked the abdomen during contractions and told Klara that everything was proceeding normally. She brought her patient some coffee to sip and a hard-boiled egg to give her energy. Then she performed a vaginal examination and called the doctor. "Klara's cervix is four centimeters dilated and almost completely effaced," she said, "and her *Wehen* [pains] are four minutes apart."

"I'll be there in about an hour," Dr. Wiesemann replied.

Erich didn't know what to do with himself. The midwife really didn't want him there; that was clear. And he had no idea how he could help Klara. He'd seen a lot of animals being born—calves, lambs, kittens, and puppies—so the process was not unfamiliar, but nobody at that time taught classes in childbirth to prospective parents, and husbands were generally banished from the whole process. As he waited during the long evening hours, sitting in the living room and hearing Klara moaning and crying, he felt helpless and scared.

Dr. Wiesemann arrived, examined Klara, and pronounced everything to be fine. Soon the second stage of labor, the pushing, began and Klara had to work in earnest. Erich was allowed to come into the bedroom and saw the head of the baby crowning, the shoulders turning, and a slick, rosy infant emerging. The doctor held the baby up by its feet and said, "It's a girl! Time of birth: ten minutes before one a.m., June 30, 1932."

"Oh, our little Brigitte is born," exclaimed Erich, full of delight, "no 'Punkel' anymore." The couple had decided to call her "Brigitte," a well-known name, meaning queen or goddess of light. There was a popular commercial to buy a certain kind of bread at that time: *"Brigitte—kauf Ullsteinschnitte!"* [Brigitte—buy Ullstein slices!] The baby's middle names were Klara (for her maternal grandmother) and Friederike (for her paternal grandmother).

"Let me hold her," Klara whispered.

"In a minute," the midwife spoke firmly. "First I want to wash Brigitte and put some clothes on her."

Klara acquiesced. After she delivered the placenta, the doctor left with instructions for Sister Marie, who was to stay in the home for two weeks. Mothers were expected to adhere to the *Wochenbett* (several weeks' bed rest), after their ordeal.

Erich and Sister Marie took many black-and-white photos, which Klara saved.

She also saved congratulatory telegrams, a good-luck *Pfennig* (penny), and some greens of the many bouquets from friends, all to go into a photo album for Brigitte. (*These photos are in my album/life book.*)

It was an exciting and exhausting time for Klara. She breast-fed her baby girl for a few weeks, rested in bed a lot, and learned diapering and formula preparation. Sister Marie was an exacting taskmistress and believed in a strict schedule for babies. "It's best to train them early," she said, "otherwise they'll get spoiled." When she left, however, Klara decided not to let the baby cry, but to pick her up. She was still worried about deviating from the schedule of feedings, but found it easier to do that than to listen to her baby cry. Since Erich had to go to work, almost all baby care was on her shoulders. She learned day by day. Cloth diapers had to be swished in the toilet when necessary, then boiled with soap in a large pot on the stove, rinsed, and finally dried on lines strung in the bathroom or, in good weather, on the balcony. (*There was no washer or dryer, no diaper service, and of course there were no disposable diapers.*) In the evenings, Erich played with his baby girl, bathed her, and often talked to her as he put her in her bassinet.

Klara started writing in the baby book/photo album/life book for the new little family member.

This album is the main source of much that I've put in quotation marks in this family chronicle. The black-and-white photos look as crisp as if they had been taken yesterday.

The new *Mutti* (Mom) wrote extensively, describing not only her daughter, but some events of the time. She called Brigitte "little Gitte" and wrote: "Today little Gitte is three weeks old. It seems that we three, Papa, Mutti, and Baby, have been together forever. Gitte is sleeping so sweetly in her white bassinet. Her hands are balled into little fists to the right and left of her head and her cute nose looks bravely into the world. May we be able to preserve this peacefulness for our dear little daughter!"

On another occasion she wrote the formula for babies at that time: "RECIPE: Take ¼ liter water and add 1 tablespoon oats. Boil for 15 minutes, strain without stirring. Add an equal amount of boiled milk and 1 teaspoon sugar. Fill a baby bottle, hold it against your eyelid to check the temperature. Make a hole in the rubber nipple and put it on the bottle. Now take Baby on your lap and speak to it encouragingly. Give the bottle. Wait lovingly and patiently until Baby deigns to drink. Don't get mad if the bottle is angrily thrown on the floor and breaks. Kiel, 1932."

As I write this early in the twenty-first century, as a grandmother of eight who often babysits, I appreciate the improvements in baby-care products. Imagine having to make your own formula, using and sterilizing glass bottles and rubber nipples without a dishwasher. Imagine not having disposable diapers and having to sanitize cloth diapers without a washer and dryer! And imagine not having formula and strained baby foods ready to buy.

Erich participated in childcare much more than was customary for men in those days. He enjoyed feeding and holding Brigitte and especially taking her on walks in her elegant pram.

Klara kept a record of Brigitte's progress: "During the first days of October our little girl, now three months old, is eagerly eating applesauce, banana pieces, and spinach with great enjoyment. She also attempts to lift her head and says 'örö-rö-rö, hah-höh.'

"Today, on the ninth of November, at age four months, Baby got her first toy, a pink-and-white rattle, which she shakes as ineptly as possible but loves to hear."

As December 31 approached, Klara and Erich decided to celebrate *Sylvester* (the German New Year's Eve celebration) quietly at home with their baby. It was a first for them both, since usually they had attended lively dance parties, sometimes in costume.

"*Na ja,*" Erich said, looking at Klara after dinner, "let's have some music and champagne and mull over the happenings of the year!"

"Ach, Erich . . ." Klara demurred, but then she did turn on the radio. The operetta *Die Fledermaus* was playing. Klara sat down on the sofa, and began. "The most important event was little Brigitte's arrival."

"No argument there. But I'm also thinking about the world at large. In physics, for instance, the discovery of the neutron was important. And Werner Heisenberg's uncertainty theory about quantum mechanics."

"Oh, now you're showing off!" replied Klara. "Well, I can add more. How about that Graf Zeppelin dirigible flying to South America? And that American woman, Amelia Earhart, flying solo over the Atlantic?"

"And now we have radio, thanks to Marconi."

Klara got up to check on the baby. When she returned, she sipped her champagne and reflected, "*Na ja,* I read some great books this year. One was *Brave New World* by Aldous Huxley. That's a frightening book about what might happen politically. And then I really liked that wonderful book about life in China by Pearl Buck, *The Good Earth.*"

I still have these books, in German, of course.

The couple sat quietly awhile, listening to music and enjoying their quiet time together. But then Erich became serious. "Our political situation is really bad. I'm afraid of a possible civil war. The communists and the conservatives are at each other's throats, and there's fighting in the streets in some cities. And that new party, the NSDAP, *die Nationalsozialistische deutsche Arbeiterpartei* [the National Socialist German Workers Party, later called the Nazis], seems to be a bunch of rowdies that are gaining support."

"Ach, Erich, let's not think about that. We're healthy, we have a beautiful baby, you have a good job, we have a home that's *gemütlich* [cozy]. We have so much to be grateful for and such a bright future ahead."

Ein gutes Neues Jahr! Happy New Year! Bonne et Heureuse Année!

Brigitte's baptism on February 26, 1933, at age eight months, was attended by Tante Johanna and Onkel Toni, visiting from Düsseldorf, and by Klara's sister, Erna, coming from Werne. Klara wrote in Brigitte's album: "Baby was appropriately serious, except for some vocal exercises, which echoed loudly through the church. The pastor gave us good words about God's great love, which also surrounds this little child with warmth. In the afternoon, during coffee hour with our relatives, Brigitte participated, to everyone's delight. We're so happy with our little Brigitte Klara Friederike."

Klara savored the baptism ritual and saved the christening gown. *I still have it, although it hasn't been worn again, since my two granddaughters were not baptized in our more secular family.*

During Erna's visit, Klara mentioned to her sister, over afternoon coffee, that she didn't remember their father at all. "In fact, I'm not even sure what he did," she said.

"Oh, I forgot; I brought you something!" Erna went to the guest room and returned with a thin folder. "I found this among mother's papers as I was sorting them out after she died."

Klara reached out, took the folder, and opened it. "Ach, look at that! Some letters from our father to our mother, Clara. How exciting!" (*Note the different spelling of the name.*)

When I found these letters among my parents' papers, it was certainly an exciting event for me! I had never heard much about the Füting side of the family. I didn't know anything about my maternal grandfather, except that he died young. These letters were written in the old Sütterling German script, on paper yellowed with age. I could not decipher everything and was grateful to have help from my aunt Maria Buchmann (Kurt's wife), when she visited from Germany, and from Ruth Budisic, an elderly friend in Michigan, so that I was able to translate the letters. I decided to insert them into the family chronicle at this point, since I have already described my paternal grandparents.

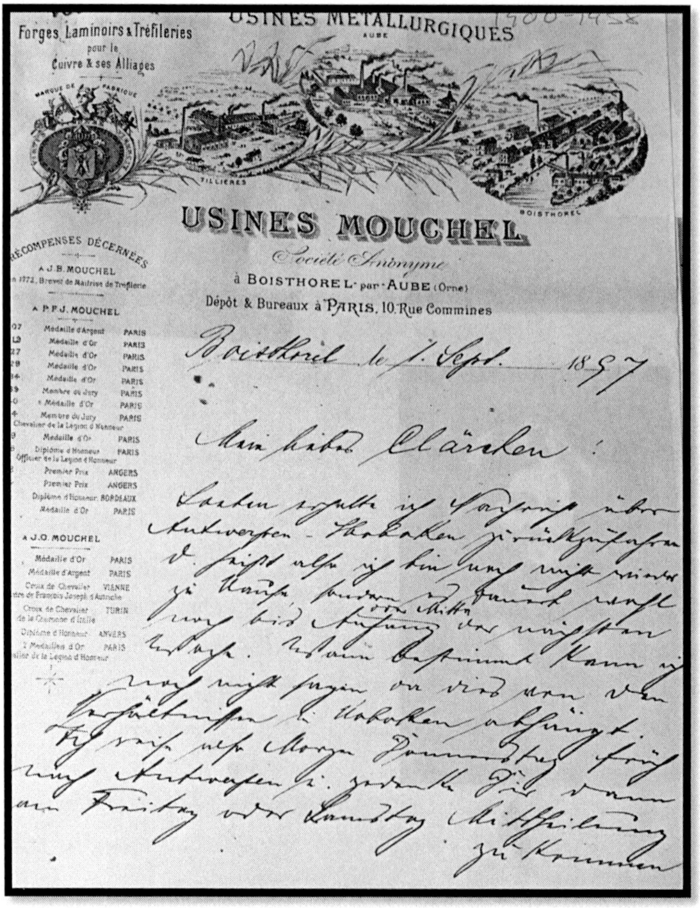
USINES METALLURGIQUES

Forges, Laminoirs & Tréfileries pour le Cuivre & ses Alliages

TILLIERES — BOISTHOREL

USINES MOUCHEL

Société Anonyme

à BOISTHOREL par AUBE (Orne)

Dépôt & Bureaux à PARIS, 10, Rue Commines

RÉCOMPENSES DÉCERNÉES

A J.B. MOUCHEL

1772, Brevet de Maîtrise de Tréfilerie

A P.F.J. MOUCHEL

Médaille d'Argent PARIS

Médaille d'Or PARIS

Médaille d'Or PARIS

Médaille d'Or PARIS

Médaille d'Or PARIS

Membre du Jury PARIS

Médaille d'Or PARIS

Membre du Jury PARIS

Chevalier de la Legion d'Honneur

Médaille d'Or PARIS

Diplôme d'Honneur PARIS

Officier de la Legion d'Honneur

Premier Prix ANGERS

Premier Prix ANGERS

Diplôme d'Honneur BORDEAUX

Médaille d'Or PARIS

A J.O. MOUCHEL

Médaille d'Or PARIS

Médaille d'Argent PARIS

Croix de Chevalier de François Joseph d'Autriche VIENNE

Croix de Chevalier de la Couronne d'Italie TURIN

Diplôme d'Honneur ANVERS

2 Médailles d'Or PARIS

Officier de la Legion d'Honneur

Boisthorel le 1. Sept. 1897

Mein liebes Clärchen!

The first letter was from Boisthorel, France, dated September 1, 1897, on paper with a very fancy letterhead in French. *Usines Metallurgiques* (Metallurgical Works) was the main heading, followed by a list of mines, forges, flattening and laminating mills, and wire-drawing mills for copper and its alloys in France and Belgium. The letter was addressed to Klara's and Erna's mother:

> *Mein liebes Clärchen!* [My dear little Clara]
>
> I just received a letter asking me to return to Antwerp-Hoboken (Belgium). That means I'm not on my way home yet; it'll probably take till the beginning or

middle of next week. When exactly I can't say with certainty, since it'll depend on the situation I find in Hoboken. I'll leave Thursday morning for Antwerp and plan to send you an update on Friday or Saturday. I'll be sorry not to see Bertha (Clara's older sister) anymore when I arrive, but I can't help it. Perhaps Bertha will decide to stay with you a little longer.

I'm really looking forward to my return and to seeing you again; and I hope to find you feeling better than when I left. Also I'm looking forward to some good German cooking. French cuisine is too bland for my taste. Can't get pea soup, sauerbraten, beer soup, or good roast potatoes. And the beer isn't much either. Well, enough for now. Hoping for a happy reunion soon.

Warm greetings and kisses, and greetings to
Bertha, also,
Your Fritz

Send any letters you may write to *Societe anonyme d'Usine de Desargentation* [Anonymous Society of the Factory for Silver Removal], *Hoboken/Antwerp.*

"Well, look at that . . ." Klara mused, "this gives us some information. At that time, I wasn't born yet. Maybe our mother was pregnant with you? And that's why she wasn't feeling well? And why her older sister Bertha was staying with her? And our Papa was nicknamed "Fritz," for Friedrich. And he traveled from our home, which at that time was in Kupfermühle, in what is Denmark now, to France and Belgium."

"Yes," Erna replied, "I think he seemed to have been consulting for these companies that mined and processed copper. I guess he was a mining engineer or metallurgist and it looks as if he was quite good and important. And—hey—our hometown name, 'Kupfermühle' [Copper Mill], implies that we lived there because of a copper mine and processing mill in that area. They probably made copper plating and wires."

Klara: "This clears up a lot of questions I had."

Erna: "Just wait 'til you see the next two letters!"

Klara folded over the papers and saw the next letter. This time the letterhead read: "Norddeutscher Lloyd, Bremen, Steamship *Bremen*." Klara read out loud what Fritz had written:

> Neapel [Naples, Italy], 2/11/1898 [the second of November, 1898], on board. Dear Clara, Ernchen [little Erna], Bertha—

"See," Klara interrupted herself, "now you have been born, Erna!" She took a sip of coffee and continued.

> Just back on board, after being on land for a while; and I feel the need to write you a few more words.
>
> Now I'm writing quickly, so that this letter can still go with the mail of the *Bremen*, which—as a Reichspost steamship—has its own post office and allows the use of German stamps, as you can see. Tonight at twelve o'clock we'll sail on. Up to now, everything has gone very nicely. Not a bit of seasickness; but then the sea has been calm until now. On board we feel quite at home, like a big family. Within this, however, special groupings are forming. Imagine, dear Clara, I met here on board some friends from Duisburg (Germany)—a married couple who are on a sightseeing tour from Genoa to Naples. There are many other nice people, including a large number of Germans, some of them nobility, and some going to Australia.
>
> The spa facilities on board, as well as the offerings for recreational use, are most luxurious. I've begun to take a saltwater bath every morning. The food is outstanding; I'm enclosing menus and other printed materials. The most fabulous scenery I've ever seen was when we entered the Gulf of Naples under sunny skies. One can see the tropical vegetation lining the panorama of the city, the Isle of Capri, and Mount Vesuvius. It's indescribably beautiful. It's too bad that you couldn't look at that with me, dear Clara. I'm thinking of you very often, dear Clara and my little darling. Our parting was very hard for me.
>
> The next docking station will be Port Said, Egypt. You can look up our arrival time in the prospectus. In case of

an emergency, contact the Agency of the Norddeutscher Lloyd and they'll deliver mail at one of the docking stations. Enough for now, my dears. The dinner bell is ringing. I hope that you are all well, as I am. Hugs and kisses to you and to my little darling, as well as to Bertha. Fritz.

Klara and Erna sat silently. A tear rolled down Klara's cheek.

"Ach, *Lieber Gott* [dear God], he sounds so loving and sweet. I wish he hadn't died so young. How good it would have been to have such a papa when we were children!"

"Yes, and our mother would probably have been more relaxed and warm, too."

I was floored when I saw the extent of my young maternal grandfather's travels. It was fascinating to compare the slow speed of travel, by train and ship, with today's air travel. And comparing the laborious communications by mail and occasional telegraph with today's phones and email, utilizing satellites, is such dramatic improvement. On the other hand, the steamship Bremen *would be luxurious even by today's standards.*

Klara mused aloud, "I've often wondered; what did Papa die of?"

Erna replied, "I've heard different accounts. Sometimes mother or one of the aunts and uncles said it was pneumonia, but a few people said it was dysentery or even malaria."

Klara: "We must have been very well off, judging by that photo of our house in Kupfermühle. It's a mansion. Did I ever show you that picture?" She jumped up and retrieved an album from the large bookcase.

"Look at that—isn't it beautiful? And the grounds are like a park! Did I tell you that Erich and I visited there during our honeymoon? We even met the old gardener, Mr. Petersen, and he remembered me taking my first steps there!"

"Well, you were born in 1901, and you were the youngest of us three girls. So father must have died around 1903. That must have been an enormous shock for mother. And apparently it was a great financial upheaval, too, because that's when we all moved to Werne in Westphalia. Mother even helped out in the shop of a friend. I guess father hadn't made any provisions; life insurance wasn't common back then. But thank God for Uncle Jakob. Mother always said her brother was the richest man in Cologne; and he helped support all of us and paid for our education. Still, Mother was always somewhat lonely and sad as I remember her. Can't blame her."

Klara looked down at her lap and said, "Wait, there's one more letter!"

This letter was written on stationery headed: "Menzies Hotel, Melbourne."

"Goodness," Klara exclaimed, "it's from Australia. Father really got around!" She read out loud:

> Melbourne, June 2, 1899. My dear Clara and little Erna,
>
> Well, I've just arrived in Melbourne and am about to depart for Sydney to board the ship to America. In Sydney I'll have a few days to see the beautiful surroundings and to prepare for the long sea voyage. I want to be sure that my stomach will be completely up to par, because the ship I'll be travelling on is very small, only 3,500 tons, compared to the *Bremen*, which was 11,000 tons. I have a mighty great respect for seasickness.
>
> I'm feeling well by now, but the first part of the journey was very, very rough, and I arrived in Adelaide quite ill. The people of the B. Mill Club [I haven't been able to determine what this was] were really nice. They gave me a *bon voyage* present—a beautiful photo album as a souvenir of B. Mill, with all the factories and mines, as well as our metal mills, and also a group photograph of all my best friends. I'm very touched by their thoughtfulness. As a goodbye gesture I hosted a champagne dinner.
>
> My dear ones, when you receive this letter I'll probably be in Vancouver (Canada). I'm hoping for good luck with this trip; and on my arrival I will use the telegraph to let you know. Telegraphy is still very expensive, though.
>
> When I eventually leave New York City for home, I'll sail on either the *Lahn* on the fifth of September, or the *Kaiser Wilhelm the Great* on the twelfth of September. The latter is the largest ship in the world and can make the trip from New York to Bremen in six and a half to seven days. [*That's fast even today.*]
>
> Well, we'll see, Clara dear! At any rate I'll send you news. By the twentieth of September I should certainly be home with you, and I'm looking forward to it enormously. I'll be happy to have our reunion. Can't wait

> to see you, my dear Clara, and my sweet little girl, Erna. You'll get more news from Sydney; then nothing for three and a half to four weeks, at least no letter. In the meantime, warm greetings and kisses to both of you.
>
> Your Papa.

Klara looked at the letterheads again. "In September 1897 our Papa went from Germany to France and Belgium. In February 1898 he's writing from Naples, Italy, and says he's going to Port Said, Egypt, next. In June 1899 he's writing from Melbourne, Australia, and says that he's going to embark in Sydney, to the port of Vancouver, Canada, next and then on to New York City, in America. He expects to be home in September, 1899. What was he doing?"

"I wish I knew," answered Erna, "but I don't recall anyone really explaining it. I guess the grown-ups knew and didn't think we children needed to be informed."

Erna added, "I have some Japanese china—a tea service—that comes from Papa. I wonder whether he was in the Orient, also." (*I have that tea set now. It is not signed, but quite pretty.*)

Klara: "It's frustrating, but, on the other hand, we were never interested and never asked questions. Do you know how Mother and Papa met?"

Erna: "No, I don't know that either."

Klara: "Well, our father seems to have been an important person and a loving and caring husband and father. It must have been hard on him and Mother, though, to have him absent so much, especially with the long delay in letters." She stood up and hugged her sister. "Thank you, Erna, for coming and for bringing these letters. Would you mind if I kept them and saved them here?"

Erna: "No, you should have them. You have a child now. These letters should be kept for the next generation. Klara, it's been so good to have a long visit with you and Erich and little Brigitte on this happy occasion."

CHAPTER 5

1933: Brigitte's development.
Hitler's rise to power. Political background. Loss of civil liberties.
Vater's (Erich's father's) death and eulogy.
Information about Mutter's (Erich's mother's) parents.

On the last day of February 1933, Brigitte turned over on the dressing table and fell off. Klara screamed in horror, picked her up, and checked her over. The baby seemed all right. But Klara was so worried that she called Erich at work and he came home immediately. Little "Gitte" appeared to be fine, except for a bump that rose on the back of her head.

I like to blame this mishap, tongue in cheek, for my lifelong difficulty in remembering people's names.

The parents thanked God that all seemed to be well. Later, as they sat down for their usual evening meal of sandwiches, hard-boiled eggs, and soup, Erich looked up and said, "You know, Kläre, I feel quite satisfied with the way we're living now, don't you?"

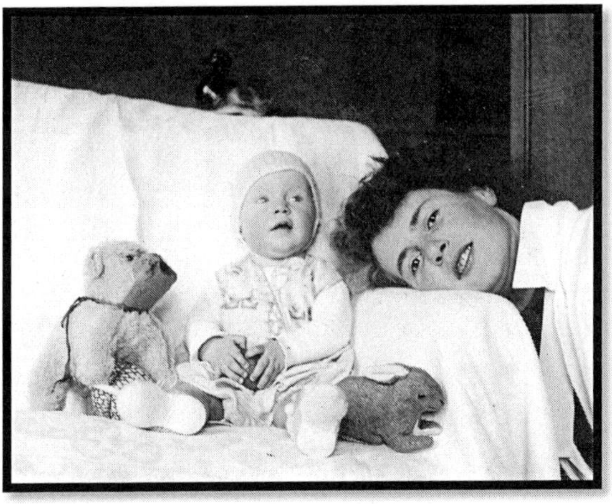

"*Ja*, of course, and I think we can especially appreciate it because we've lived through a war in our teens, a war which our fatherland lost, and then that hyperinflation and depression."

"We've had to work very hard," continued Erich, "and we certainly didn't have much to start with, but we had our educations and we've held jobs all along. And now we have our happy little family, a secure income, and a healthy baby. I'm very grateful."

Neither of them had an inkling of the storm clouds gathering on the horizon of their existence, bringing war and destruction in their future.

Klara got excited one day, as she was wheeling her baby through some garden paths, when suddenly little Brigitte clearly said, "Mama." Back home, Klara noted this in the photo album and added, "Brigitte stands up by herself. April 1933." Many developmental milestones happened in May: Brigitte learned to walk, holding onto the playpen sides, said "Papa" quite clearly, and showed four teeth. "In the mornings our little Gitte sits on the potty and does her big job. But during the day? No success yet. Brigitte loves to eat the dirt from the potted palm. She also thinks it's great fun to stand at the kitchen sink and splash." The daily changes and advances of their one-year-old toddler held endless fascination for Klara and Erich.

Klara now had a mother's helper, a young woman called Emma. She was putting in her year as *Pflichtjahrmädchen* (duty-year girl), a one-year service required by the government for young women. (*Young men had to join the Hitler Youth or serve in other ways.*) Emma bought the groceries, while mother and daughter took their morning outing, and she also helped with the housework and laundry. Klara liked to dress well for her walks and Erich took some lovely photos, which Klara put into Brigitte's album. Fashions had changed; dresses were longer again, down to the lower calf, and the bosom was no longer compressed, but emphasized. (*By the way: a similar change from short to long skirts occurred in the late forties and early fifties. It was started by Dior and called "The New Look."*) Klara was proud of her fox fur, worn around the shoulders. The fox's snout had a clamp that held the fur around the neck, while the fluffy tail hung down. This was the height of fashion and little Brigitte loved to play with it.

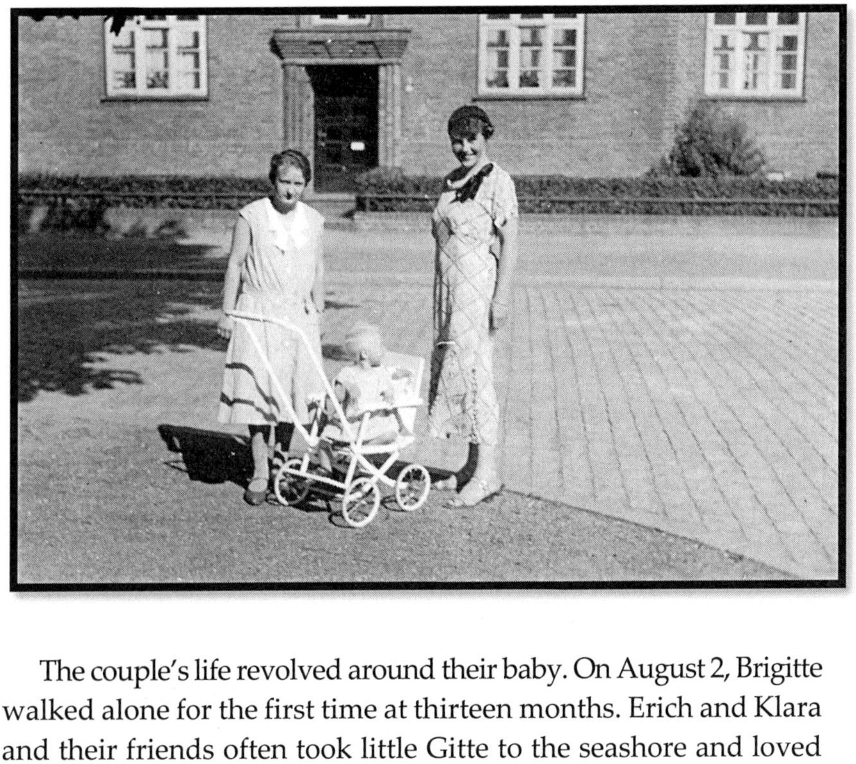

The couple's life revolved around their baby. On August 2, Brigitte walked alone for the first time at thirteen months. Erich and Klara and their friends often took little Gitte to the seashore and loved watching her play in the sand and water. At home she started climbing everywhere: onto the desk, the windowsill, the sofa, and every chair.

Erich was doing well at the research station, but didn't discuss his work at home. Most men kept their work and home life separate.

Away from home, life in Germany was somewhat less chaotic than it had been. The leader of the National Socialist German Workers Party, the NSDAP, was Adolf Hitler. He had become chancellor of Germany on January 30, 1933, through some clever backroom political maneuvering. Hitler was an Austrian who had served as a corporal in the German army during World War I (1914–18) and found himself disillusioned and disappointed after Germany's defeat. He tried to succeed as an artist, but did better as a fledgling politician. After a political brawl in Munich, he had been imprisoned and wrote a book, *Mein Kampf* (*My Struggle*), in which he blamed traitors at home for the defeat of the noble army. He particularly singled out Jews as undermining the country.

After becoming chancellor, a huge torchlight parade in Berlin celebrated the occasion. It was a spectacular demonstration, with uniforms, flags, marches, and music. However, in Kiel, this didn't have much impact.

Hitler's cabinet included Hermann Göring, age forty, a dashing, former air force ace who had been commander of the *Richthoven* (the Red Baron) fighter squadron in the war and had shot down twenty-two Allied aircraft. Those small planes during the war of 1914–1918 had open cockpits, and pilots on both sides could see one another as they attacked. The German and English aviators actually had great respect for each other, and the air war was a game of bravery and chivalry among elite young pilots. Göring was charming and cultured. His Danish wife, the Baroness Karin von Fock-Kanzow, had just died the year before of tuberculosis and he was still grieving. He was appointed *Reichsmarshall* (president of the *Reichstag,* the parliament) and commander-in-chief of the *Luftwaffe* (the air force).

On February 5, 1933, Hitler named Dr. Joseph Göbbels, age thirty-five, Reich minister for propaganda and popular enlightenment. He also became president of the Reich culture chamber. Göbbels controlled radio and newspapers, the main sources of information in those days before television and the internet. He also censored magazines, books, films, and all cultural life, including theater, music, and dance. It was his mission to strengthen the new government, to let successes be reported extensively, and to suppress news of dissent.

At first the government's tighter control was welcomed, since many people were tired of the ineffectual and weak Weimar republic, where literally dozens of parties squabbled with each other and little was done for the suffering country and its people, especially unemployment. The violent street fights and riots among the communists, the various Christian democratic parties, and the NSDAP were dangerous to citizens. Hitler promised decisive action to improve the deplorable situation in Germany, and Göbbels saw to the publicity for the new leadership.

Based on what Klara wrote in her diary and the photo albums, neither Erich nor Klara, nor most of their friends, were particularly interested in politics. However, talking about the situation in the country one night, Erich said, "This Hitler has continued implementing the Public Works Corps. They're recruiting unemployed men to build an Autobahn and work on other infrastructure rebuilding."

The autobahn became a model for rapid-travel highways in many countries.

"Well, that's a very good idea," replied Klara. "Remember how many of those young men I saw out of work, loitering in the park when I was pregnant with Brigitte?"

Erich responded, "Yes, there's improvement. I've also read that the new president in America, Franklin Delano Roosevelt, is following the idea and doing something very similar to alleviate their severe unemployment that started in the Depression. His PWA, or Public Works Administration, puts men to work on national parks and bridges and such, and even pays musicians and artists."

Unfortunately, in both countries the leaders later also boosted employment by another proven method, that of military buildup—Hitler in the 1930s and Roosevelt in the 1940s.

Occasionally, Erich and Klara would enjoy a glass of wine after their dessert and, after taking a sip while reading the paper one evening, Erich looked up and told Klara, "I see that in America the great experiment of banning alcohol has failed. Prohibition has been repealed."

With increasing employment, the German economy improved and people became more optimistic. Hitler's administration at this time also started the *Hitlerjugend* (Hitler Youth) for boys and the *Bund deutscher Mädchen*, or *BDM* (Association of German Girls). These groups played sports, sang patriotic songs, hiked, learned nature lore and crafts, and hailed Hitler. Young people were occupied and kept out of trouble.

On February 27, 1933, the *Reichstag* (Parliament building) burned in Berlin. It was thought initially that the communists were responsible, and many citizens feared civil war. (*Later the fire was attributed to a young man, who may have been mentally ill.*) Hitler asked the president, respected older politician Graf von Hindenburg, to sign an "emergency decree for the protection of the German people" as, unfortunately, allowed by the new constitution. This decree effectively suspended the constitution and civil rights, as well as freedom of the press.

There was now a ban on all opinions that would put the administration in a bad light. Moderate newspapers were closed, public meetings suspended. All local governments were dissolved and power shifted to provincial management. Now most police and judicial power was concentrated in Prussia, the province in which Berlin is located. The National Socialist German Workers Party had emerged from the jumble of over thirty parties as the dominant one. Domestic terror had begun.

It is frightening, in retrospect, to see how fast many civil liberties were lost. It took only one month to commence! I had some fears of similar developments when President Bush invaded Iraq. Suddenly people who opposed this policy were labeled unpatriotic in the press and by others.

Some political enemies, especially communists, but also Protestant Lutheran leaders, professors, and Jews, were imprisoned at Dachau, which was designated as an *Arbeitslager* (work camp) for German political prisoners. The Catholic clergy generally did not protest the Nazi policies. Pacelli, the Vatican secretary of state, who later became Pope Pius XII, had negotiated the *Reich Concordat* with Hitler. German Catholic leaders were to withdraw from social and political action in Germany. In return, Hitler granted financial compensation and tolerance. Catholics represented approximately half of the population, mainly in the south. The other main religious sector, mostly in Northern Germany, was Protestantism. Most large Lutheran churches mouthed pious, patriotic platitudes and did not address either the suffering of the people or the oppression by official government policies. But there were exceptions, and the best-known among them was Paul Tillich, who had been a war (World War I) hero and who spoke out about the suppression of free speech and the anti-Semitic rhetoric. As a consequence, he was suspended from his post as head of the philosophy faculty in Frankfurt. Erich and Klara liked the writings of Tillich and were quite worried about these new developments.

The government had by this time developed a powerful propaganda machine. No other country had as effective an "advertising executive" as Göbbels. He often did not use any actual lies, just emphasis of certain news items and suppression of others. All the news reports in papers and on radio were positive with regard to the party and the government's actions. Criticism was considered unpatriotic and traitorous. (*I think Göbbels was the first great Spin Master.*)

The people of Germany now had to be careful about what they said and to whom. Even neighbors could become informants. The time of *Flüsterwitze* (whispered jokes) began. "Yes, I'm Aryan. I'm blond like Hitler [who was dark], tall like Göbbels [who was short and had a limp], and slender like Göring [who had become fat]."

Racial purity was an important topic at this time. Hitler's administration advocated keeping the "Aryan race" (Northern Europeans, Indians, and Persians) "uncontaminated" by avoiding admixture with Jews, Eastern Europeans, Gypsies, Asians, American Indians, or Australian aborigines. Of course, this goal was not original to or limited to German ideologists. Quite a few theorists in Europe, England, and the United States advocated similar views.

In Germany, citizens applying for many highly desirable positions, such as government and university appointments, now had to fill out an *Ahnenpass* (a passport of ancestors), listing their parents and grandparents and their religions. (*I have one of these that belonged to my uncle.*) These listings had to be certified by local civil or religious officials. Anyone not "racially pure" was ineligible for consideration. In this way the encroachment on the rights of Jews and certain other ethnic groups increased. But, as often happens, social and political changes proceeded in almost imperceptible increments so that the general public was not acutely aware of the continuing loss of liberties. Citizens were much more aware of the significant progress in civil order, economic health, and general optimism.

On December 20, 1933, the Buchmanns received a telegram from Erich's mother, reading: "*VATER SCHWER KRANK SOFORT KOMMEN—MUTTER*" [Vater seriously ill; come immediately; Mutter]. This was unexpected and sad news. Erich's father, Johann Wilhelm Buchmann, had contracted an *E. coli* infection following prostate surgery. It was called blood poisoning and very serious. (*There were no antibiotics available at that time.*) Erich hid his emotions outwardly by calmly organizing their trip, but Klara expressed hers by sobbing and crying. The two and their baby, Brigitte, immediately set out on a long train trip that very night. But when they arrived in Voerde, they learned that Vater Johannn had died an hour earlier! He was only sixty-nine years old.

The family stayed in Voerde for two weeks and little Brigitte, one and a half years old, became the darling of numerous uncles and aunts, as well as cousins.

One afternoon Klara had the opportunity to talk quietly with her mother-in-law, Friederike. She asked about Mutter's parents. Friederike said, "*Na ja,* it's an interesting story. My mother was called Elise Steinkamp and she came from Damm, near Wesel, in the *Dämmerwald* [dusky woods]. She inherited a farm after her older sister died. My father, Johann Weyer, had been courting her for a while and she had fallen in love with him, too. But when it turned out that she now had inherited the farm, then her mother wanted her to marry a rich farmer's son, to combine the two farms. That man had originally planned to marry the older sister, but when she died he became interested in Elise. However, my mother stuck by her choice and married Johann Weyer for love. The couple settled in the farm, which was in Havelich, near Brünen. Well, my poor father, Johann, was never able to make any decisions about running the farm because his mother-in-law still ran everything with a firm hand and strict regimen.

"And she lived to a very old age! You can imagine that this put quite a strain on the marriage, but I always felt that my parents lived together in a very warm and loving relationship."

Klara was glad to have learned more about the family. Later on, she and Erich took Brigitte to Düsseldorf to spend some time with Tante Johanna and Onkel Toni.

After their return to Kiel, Erich sat down at his big desk in the living room to write *A Memoir of Vater*. He wanted to eulogize his father and pulled out papers, letters, and photos to include in the manuscript.

I have translated his memoir as follows:

"My Vater was born on November 12, 1864, on the farm called Kreblingshof in the village of Brünen. [About this time in the US Civil War, the Union General William T. Sherman burned Atlanta where I am now writing this family history.] Vater was baptized Johann Wilhelm [John William]. When he was growing up his grandfather still lived there, retired from farm work, sitting by the tiled oven, smoking a pipe, wearing a cap on his head, and still controlling everything that went on, from farm procedures to the education of his grandchildren. The five grandchildren vied for the opportunity to lead the cow to graze along the grassy edge of the road. That would earn them a 'present,' which often consisted of just a slice of bread with butter.

"Johann's father was strict, but apparently did not influence his son's life greatly. He died when Vater was only twenty-eight. His mother, however, was very influential with all her children and the entire Buchmann family. She was born Helene Margarethe Tinnefeld on December 1, 1833, and died on December 17, 1901, at the age of sixty-eight. Although she, too, was embedded in the constrictive mores of Brünen, she was able to teach others to think about deeper implications of the strict Christianity that was practiced there. She enabled Vater and many others to free themselves from the excesses of having to think and do 'as it has always been.'"

Erich had visited the farm in Brünen often as a child and remembered much about his relatives and other inhabitants of the village. He wrote, "Everything was done according to long-standing custom. Everyone considered him- and herself very important and spoke and acted in a rather regal manner. A teenager, walking with adults, would imitate their slow and considered speech and actions, shaking his head thoughtfully, and he would be taken seriously. Much discussion concerned other family members, and all their actions were discussed at length. Although such scrutiny and gossip were sometimes oppressive, the flip side was that everyone who had trouble or needs was immediately helped with great generosity.

"When Vater was eleven years old, there was an epidemic of diarrhea and fever in the village. Two of his ten siblings died, and the sadness of these deaths stayed with him for life.

"Social life in Brünen was stratified according to the size and wealth of the farms. The *Grossbauern* [large-farm owners] kept to themselves, even during big village festivals. Everyone accepted that this was the way the world worked.

"Vater was the fifth child and second son in his family and worked on one of the large farms [in Brünen]. Later he was drafted, and upon his return he married Friederike Weier [*sometimes spelled Weyer*] on November 14, 1894. He later learned dairy management and moved to Voerde [*sometimes spelled Vörde*]. He and Friederike [*Mutter*] both worked as hard as their employees and enlarged the dairy functions. By 1912, they already had nine children, and Mutter was too busy to help in the business.

"At about this time a neighbor, called Dietrich Dehnen, invited Vater and Mutter to his house, where a group of people held a one-hour Bible study every week. This affirmed a strong belief by Vater in the love and mercy of God, so that he felt certain that every happening was ordained by God and that God could be trusted to set everything right. He had an almost childlike trust in the leadership of God in all his affairs, which served him well all his life.

"When the war [*World War I*] started in 1914, Vater was forty-nine years old and his oldest son, Hans, was twelve. Since many of their employees were drafted, this was a time of extremely hard work for everyone who was left. In addition, Vater was in charge of the distribution of rationed groceries and butter for the village, which caused problems with some people. But he managed to keep calm and be fair, largely because of his faith in God.

"One year after the war ended in 1918 the last child, Helmut, was born. He was the fifteenth child, of which thirteen survived. Vater continued to work diligently in his office, always at a standing desk. He was a hard negotiator with his customers. In the evenings, he read the paper and discussed the latest news over dinner. He was a strict monarchist and believed that royalty was ordained by God. He supported the Kaiser. [*Wilhelm II, 1859–1941, first child of Queen Victoria and first cousin of King George II and Nicholas, Tsar of Russia. The Kaiser was forced to abdicate in 1918 after World War I*]. Nevertheless, he criticized any poor political management.

"The biggest goal and challenge in Vater's life was to fulfill his ambition to give each child a higher education. We can imagine the sacrifices required to achieve this goal with so many children studying at the same time. It was in the 1920s that, next to their house, the Buchmanns built another house, a jewel of a house, with lots of room for the big family. Vater continued with his frenzied work style, even when the oldest son, Hans, began to take over many of the management functions. But slowly Vater began to develop an interest in his large garden area, planted trees and flowers, and allowed himself some leisure. It is a pity that he was taken so suddenly. He died early on the morning of December 21, 1933, at the age of sixty-nine, in the firm belief that he would join Jesus in God's heaven. He was buried in the cemetery of Stockum with many mourners attending."

Erich included a letter written by Vater on May 3, 1931. It begins:

"Dear Erich, Dear Klara, today is the most beautiful of all days which God gives us, because he loves us." Later it continues, "It's Sunday afternoon and Mutter and I have just returned from the *Stunde* [*the hour's Bible study*]. We have just sent you a little birthday gift [*Erich's birthday was June 18*] . . . Let me have your opinion about Kurt [*Erich's younger brother*]. I think he might study in Bonn for two years and then perhaps continue in Kiel, if you two could give him room and board."

Vater continued writing about other children and events, and the letter goes on. "I hope Ernst will finish his studies soon. Can you help him find a position? [Ernst was studying physics.] Hermann still doesn't know what he wants to do. [*He later became an Oberschule—college—professor*.] It was so nice when you were all little and still here with us. Now you're all fledglings who have left the nest, and sometimes we're here all alone on a Sunday evening . . . I suppose your honeymoon time is over and now love becomes more clarified. May God be gracious to all of us. Warm greetings from the heart, Your Vater."

Finally, Erich wrote a short distillation of his father's *Weltanschauung* (world view/philosophy of life and religion), as he had heard so often:

"In the beginning God-father lived with his son in such splendor and clarity that we cannot begin to imagine it. Then God decided, in his majesty and omnipotence, to perform a magnificent act of creation and form the world. He made humans in his image. But then came the first fall. Humans ate from the tree of knowledge, breaking God's law. Now they were banished from paradise and from access to God. But God had mercy and made covenants with humanity, after the flood, with Abraham, with the children of Israel, with the commandments. But not until the son came to earth and gave himself as sacrifice on Golgatha was humanity reunited with God. In the son of God our sins were forgiven and we all can find access to God. In Jesus's name we can again say, '*Abba,* dear father.' The old covenant is superseded by the new one.

"We didn't contribute anything to this reunion with God; he alone gave us salvation. We only need to approach him with childlike hearts and seek salvation and we already have it."

Erich's memoir ends by saying that his father's faith and mythology (*sic*) gave him the strength to lead a good life and influence many people besides his large family.

CHAPTER 6

1934 and 1935: Home life. Historical background. 6/30/1936: Ulrich's birth. Olympics.

Klara and Erich invited his mother, Friederike, to visit them, to help divert her from dwelling on the sudden, unexpected loss of her husband, the father of her fifteen children. (*In a brown, leather-bound guest book, which I found among my parents' papers, Friederike wrote in part, "In May I spent several weeks with my children in Kiel. We took lovely walks, showing me Kiel's attractions, especially at the* Förde *[the beach resort area near the Baltic Sea]. These days will be a beautiful memory for me . . . Your Mutter."*)

The young couple was totally absorbed by their home life, work, and their little toddler and paid little attention to the political scene. However, they were disturbed when they read about the Lutheran ministers they admired, Dietrich Bonhoeffer, along with Karl Barth and Martin Niemöller, all preaching and writing against the new NSDAP party's regime and Adolf Hitler. Klara and Erich basically agreed with these dissenters, but felt helpless to do anything more specific.

They were also amazed when Hitler apparently condoned the killing of his old SA (*Sturm Abteil,* colloquially known as Brown Shirts) buddy, Captain Röhm, and allowed the SS (*Schutz Staffel*), under Göring and Heinrich Himmler, to become more powerful. The SS uniforms, black with a death's head or skull detail, inspired fear.

Klara continued chronicling little Brigitte's achievements in her album: "During a heavy storm the wind was howling around the house. Brigitte was listening intently and then she announced, 'It's a doggie!' Gitte is now toilet trained and when, on our walks, she sees a dog lifting his leg against a tree she says, 'Uh-uh—no, no!'" (*It's clear to me that toilet training was certainly pursued more vigorously in those days before disposable diapers.*)

Klara wrote, on another occasion: "March 1934. Tonight, after everything was quiet, I was leafing through a book of my favorite poet, Annette von Droste-Hülshoff, when I found this quote, which to me is the essence of our task of raising a child: 'Place great care on the education of the mind, the firming of character, and the refinement of manners and lifestyle.' It'll be my motto."

That March, Erich mentioned at the dinner table, "Kläre, Germany has taken back the demilitarized zone of the Rhineland. The French have left." Both Erich and Klara were glad about this news of their homeland. Like other Germans and, in fact, even some British, Americans, and others, they had never agreed that Germany was at fault in the war (World War I)—it was only honoring its treaties.

This war, which started after the assassination of the Archduke Francis Ferdinand, heir to the Habsburg throne of the Austro-Hungarian Empire, and his wife, could and should never have happened. The assassins were young Bosnian men, mostly high school students, protesting conditions in Bosnia/Serbia. It was only one episode of many assassinations at that time in history. The war, which didn't start until two months after the assassination, finally involved many nations in an attempt to preserve the balance of power in Europe. After the United States entered the war, Germany and its allies lost. This horrible war, fought in trenches and introducing the use of mustard gas, killed 20 million people. It was later deemed "the war to end all wars."

I wish that had been true.

During the fighting, troops were led by officers still using techniques of the Napoleonic era. They ordered their men to advance out of the trenches, and these poor soldiers were mowed down by new artillery weapons, such as machine guns. Sometimes fighting continued for months, with the loss of hundreds of young men, over just a few yards of territory. In the end, everyone was disillusioned on both sides. US President Wilson's "making the world safe for democracy" didn't ring true anymore. The humiliating Versailles treaty, after Germany's surrender, with its impositions of blame and outrageous demands for reparations, threw Germany's economy and fledgling democracy into disastrous conditions and eventually paved the way for the coming of totalitarianism. In addition, the French occupation of the industrial area of the Rhineland made it impossible for Germany to produce enough steel to fulfill the conditions of the treaty.

I found no reference to any of those historical details in my parents' papers, but have added them to fill in the background of the times.

Erich and Klara always liked to talk during and after dinner. Once they discussed the new president in America, Franklin Delano Roosevelt (FDR), who had started the PWA (Public Works Administration). He also began the American Social Security program, similar to the one that had already been instituted in Germany in the late 1800s by Bismarck. Unfortunately, he didn't begin universal health insurance, which Bismarck had also started in Germany at the same time. FDR encouraged his citizens and said, in his inaugural address, "The only thing we have to fear is fear itself."

On another occasion Erich and Klara talked about recent progress in medicine. Cortisone had been isolated and also testosterone. On the social front, AA (Alcoholics Anonymous) had been started.

Klara continued to write in her daughter's photo/life album. "Résumé of little Brigitte on her second birthday, June 30, 1934," she noted, writing as if Brigitte herself had dictated. "I'm now two years old. Mutti [Mom] wants me to report on my last year. That won't even fit on these couple of pages! First of all, I can talk now—and how! All day long I have conversations with Papa, Mutti, Onkuta [Uncle Kurt], Lotte [the maid], *Wauwau* [a dog], and *Balla* [a ball]. And I talk with the sea gulls on the beach and the chickens in the country. And you should see me climb! From the couch to the windowsill, onto Papa's tummy, on his face, on Onkuta's shoulder, just missing the chandelier. Papa hopes to enter me in the Olympics in 1936.

"You should have seen my birthday table—so many presents and goodies to eat. But I didn't get to eat many myself; there were so many visitors. I had to be ready, washed and combed and wearing a starched birthday dress, to come into the living room and greet every one of the seven visiting ladies in the morning, holding Lotte's hand. And Lotte was wearing a cap and an apron. And then I had to curtsy and shake hands with everyone. It was awful. At least in the afternoon one of the next three visitors brought a little boy and we could play on the floor. We also got strawberry shortcake.

"Papa and Mutti bought a wild, loud, terrifying beast. Lotte goes around all the rooms with it and I have to hide . . . Aunt Erna [Klara's sister] is coming soon and staying here with me so that Mutti and Papa can go on vacation."

I have a detailed photo album of the wonderful, picturesque places they visited throughout Germany.

"Onkuta will also be here and he keeps me in training, just like he's training in boot camp. He really does have boots . . . Here's a picture of me. Mutti used to be on it, too, but she didn't like the way she looked, so she cut herself off. Am I going to be vain like that when I grow up?"

Klara inserted many beach photos from a nearby resort, Dänisch-Nienhof, showing Brigitte in the sand, Erich in the dunes, and herself in a boy-cut, one-piece, black wool bathing suit in the surf. (*The Buchmann family would again be in Dänisch-Nienhof after World War II, under very different circumstances!*)

Erich's brother Kurt was now living with the family for a couple of years while studying at Kiel University. He also had to put in his time in basic training. He fit in well with the young family.

On October 1, 1934, Erich was promoted to *Regierungsrat* (a higher civil service grade). Klara rehearsed Brigitte: "Now, when Papa comes in the door this evening, you give him this bouquet of violets and say, '*Gratulierung* (congratulations), Papa!'" When the moment arrived, Brigitte stuck out the flowers and just said, "Here!"

This is my own very first memory:

> *The air was fresh and cool, even a little too cool. We were outdoors. I was wedged between Papa's back and Mutti's chest and I felt excited. We were going somewhere! An adventure! The sky was wide, light blue, and clear, and on my left it was streaked with rosy orange. Later I learned that I was two years old at this time, because Erich and Klara sold their motorcycle in the fall of 1934.*

According to Klara's entries, Christmas was entirely geared to little Brigitte. On December 5, she put a shoe on the windowsill and by morning St. Nicholas had filled it with candy and an apple. For the whole period of advent, Gitte talked about the *Weihnachtsmann* (Santa Claus), the Christmas tree, and the doll carriage she had requested. When Christmas Eve arrived, and Brigitte was finally allowed into the living room, holding Mutti's and Lotte's hands, she saw the Christmas tree, with flickering real candles and Papa standing next to it. On the table nearby there were lots of presents, unwrapped as customary. But Brigitte said, with disappointment, "Where's Santa?" She had expected him in person. However, soon she was busy putting her dolls into the carriage, taking them out again and in again, unpacking the blocks and putting them into the carriage, out again, in again. Later she sat on her Papa's lap and sang with him, "O *Tantenbaum*, O *Tantenbaum* . . ." (A play on words by Erich, who delighted in these games. Instead of *Tannenbaum* [fir tree], Erich sang *Tantenbaum* [Auntietree].)

Klara continued to write in her daughter's album and inserted many pictures. (*These black-and-white photos, as sharp now, in the early twenty-first century, as they were in 1934, show lively parents, many visitors, and a little towheaded, smiling toddler.*)

On Brigitte's third birthday, June 30, 1935, Klara wrote, "She liked her harmonica best and has been playing it for us all day, only putting it down to eat. We went to the beach and returned on the streetcar, much to Gitte's delight. A nice 'uncle' gave her two huge strawberries from his basket. Brigitte is now an independently thinking and acting little person, full of mischief, happy and sunny. Oh, our little *Schnuppertierchen* [snuffling little animal, "snufflebunny"], *Tinne* [Brigitte's name for herself], *Halunke* [troublemaker]!"

It is disconcerting to read about all the time, effort, energy, and care expended on parenting for me, of which I have no memory. And now my children tell me the same thing!

For four weeks the young parents and their three-year-old daughter visited relatives in Düsseldorf, Voerde, and Werne. On the way back, Brigitte got quite sick. Erich and Klara had to stop in Hamburg and call an ambulance, but everything turned out all right. (*The cause of the illness is not mentioned.*) Back in Kiel, Brigitte began to eat a little better, much to her mother's relief. She got the scooter she'd wanted for quite a while, and zoomed around on the street with her little friend Günther, under the supervision of the maid.

On September 9, Klara took little Brigitte for the first time to participate in the Lantern Game. At dusk, many children came and formed a parade in the park, holding a lantern on a stick with a lit candle in it, singing as they walked,

Laterne, Laterne,	Lantern, lantern,
Sonne, Mond, und Sterne,	Sun, moon, and stars,
Brenne auf, mein Licht,	Burn high, my light,
Brenne auf, mein Licht,	Burn high, my light,
Aber meine liebe Laterne nicht.	But don't burn up my lantern.

Brigitte was now allowed to play outside alone with her scooter after being reminded by Mutti, "No farther than the corner, stay on the sidewalk!" Mutti would look out the window from time to time. (*It seems quite remarkable to me that a toddler would be allowed out on a city street alone at that time.*)

On Christmas Eve, Gitte sang along with Papa and Mutti. She was attentive and quiet, looking at the nativity scene, when her papa read the Christmas gospel. But suddenly she broke in, "Look, look, that little sheep has its tail broken off!"

During January and February 1936, at age three and a half, Brigitte and her parents spent a full four weeks in Voerde with her *Oma* [grandmother], and in Düsseldorf with Tante Johanna and Onkel Toni. She was thoroughly spoiled and adored by them, but spoiled them right back with lots of love and hugs and kisses. Coming home, little Brigitte had a severe attack of chicken pox; the "*Onkel Doktor*" visited the home often.

The following episode was related by Klara to her eighteen-year-old grandson Eddy. She was in her eighties and he took an oral history from her.

"One day, in May 1936, I had a visitor in police uniform. When he came to the door I was a little uneasy. He was polite but he asked me, 'What newspaper do you get?' I said, 'The *Kieler Neueste Nachrichten* [*Kiel Latest News*]; we've always taken that and I write a travel column for it every weekend.' The uniformed man said, 'Don't you get the *Völkischer Beobachter* [*Folk Observer*]?' I knew that it was the official party paper, full of propaganda. I answered, not quite truthfully, 'Yes, we buy that from time to time, too, and practically every Saturday.' That seemed to appease the man. But then he asked, 'Did you put the flag out on the twentieth of April?' That was Hitler's birthday. I told him, 'No, I didn't. My husband was on a business trip, and you can see my condition; I'm pregnant and the wooden flagpole is very heavy.' He saw that and excused himself as he left."

On May 18, a very pregnant Klara wrote, "Brigitte is very happy about the expected baby, which will arrive in five to six weeks. She knows that the baby is made by God in heaven and will be brought by 'Tante Faust,' the midwife, in a suitcase. She thinks the baby is for her; Mutti can help take care of it, though."

Klara continued to write articles for various newspapers and magazines. She saved one, published in the newspaper *Kieler Neueste Nachrichten* on Sunday, June 21, 1936, which she pasted into Brigitte's album. In it she described visiting several German villages, whose ancient cottages were carefully preserved. The villagers also still preserved much of their old-fashioned lifestyle, which Klara felt had some advantages compared to the hectic and materialistic way of city dwellers.

On June 30, 1936, Brigitte had her fourth birthday. According to Klara's notes, at 6:00 a.m., her four candles were quickly lit, she was allowed to have some hot chocolate, and then she was brought, barefoot and in her nightgown, to a neighbor upstairs, along with her new toy wheelbarrow. Klara had gone into labor.

Later that evening, at six p.m., Brigitte received another present: her little brother, Ulrich (OOL-rich) Johann Buchmann! The name Ulrich was chosen by the parents because they liked it; Johann referred to his paternal grandfather. Little Ulrich would usually be called "Uli" (OOL-lee).

Isn't it amazing that my brother was born on the same day as I, in the same apartment, four years later? I have a memory of this day: I was at Tante Janssen's. Her little boy, Harald, had graduated to a bed, and Tante Janssen put me into his old crib. I didn't like being caged like that. Everything was strange here; I felt anxious and uneasy.

Later, Klara wrote this in her daughter's album: "Brigitte's sayings: 'Is Uli a boy or my brother? Look, he's so cute! He kicks his legs and his hands. Mutti, when he and I were still in heaven, you were so alone, weren't you?'"

1936 was the year when the Olympics were held in Berlin. (*In the United States we hear much about the talented African American runner, Jesse Owens. He was actually substituted by the American officials for a Jewish American athlete. They did this to avoid offending Hitler and felt that, since the Americans were expected to excel in track and field, it wouldn't affect the outcome significantly.*) Most of the other events were dominated by German athletes and the Olympics were a huge public relations and foreign policy success for Germany and Hitler.

Also in 1936: the Italian leader, il Duce Benito Mussolini, who was on good terms with Hitler, invaded Abyssinia (Ethiopia). (*I found none of such political events and comments in the many albums and notes by Klara and Erich. However, I'll keep inserting information occasionally as background.*)

Erich had to serve eight weeks of military duty for the navy in November and December. Little four-year-old Brigitte was happy when her papa came home and she admired his winter navy uniform, a dark, marine-blue one. However, she admired her own new herringbone black-and-white winter coat even more. A photo of Papa holding up Brigitte so they could look at each other nose to nose was taken by Klara.

One day, all of Brigitte's dolls disappeared. Mutti said, "Little angels came from heaven to get them and make new clothes for them for Christmas."

On Christmas Eve, Brigitte was the big girl who was allowed to attend the Lutheran church with her parents. She sang along eagerly with all the Christmas carols and later enjoyed her presents, including her newly dressed dolls.

CHAPTER 7

1937: Family Life.
1938: Brigitte starts school.
"Peace in Our Time."

When little Ulrich was baptized on January 31, 1937, Brigitte walked up to the front of the church in a very dignified manner and was proud of being the big sister. She had just learned to tie a bow, and during the party after the ceremony, she went around and untied and tied everyone's shoelaces.

From an entry by Klara into her daughter's album: "In March 1937 Brigitte came running in from playing outside and yelled, 'Mutti, what are those men doing outside?'

"'What men?'

"'Those men with the big, round googly eyes and ugly snouts! And there's a dead man on a stretcher, but he's not really dead, he gets up and talks.'

"I thought, *What can this be?* I looked out of the window and saw an anti-air-raid practice in the park across the street, with men wearing gas masks."

A full page of humorous anecdotes Klara had written about Brigitte was published in a women's magazine. Klara pasted that page into Brigitte's album. One of the little stories Klara had reported was this: "Brigitte is running on the street and bumps into a young soldier. He smiles at her and moves her over gently, saying, 'Well, what's the hurry, little one?' But he hasn't reckoned with Brigitte. She straightens up, outraged, and answers, 'I'm not little anymore. I can go potty all by myself!'" Another vignette read, "Brigitte has been visiting her Oma in the Rhineland. She has always seen her in long, dark dresses. One day she's watching her change and bursts out, 'Oma, you have legs?'"

On April 21, Brigitte didn't come home on time. Klara, with Minna, the maid at that time, searched for her desperately. Klara called Erich and he advised her to notify the police immediately, even before he could get home. She called and later saved the police report in Brigitte's album: "Runaway since noon, a four-year-old girl, light blond hair, blue eyes, blue coat, suede shoes. Has a scooter."

Shortly afterward, Brigitte calmly arrived home and told her distraught parents, "I met a new friend; her name is Elke and she lives around the corner. She's on the fourth floor and they have a balcony." Although Klara felt that her daughter deserved a spanking, her papa intervened.

Eastertime meant the measles for Brigitte, and shortly thereafter also for her little brother, Uli (Ulrich).

I remember this: I was lying in Mutti's and Papa's big bed, because I was sick. The light came in from the windows on the right and bothered my eyes. I had little red spots all over my skin. Mutti closed the drapes and that was better. Sometimes she carried me around in her arms on a big pillow.

Erich and Klara continued to be concerned about the news of the Lutheran ministers they admired. Dietrich Bonhoeffer had been banned from speaking in public. Martin Niemöller, pastor of a church in a wealthy Berlin suburb, had founded the *bekennende Kirche* (confessional church) three years ago and had been preaching antigovernment doctrine. It had all the more impact since he had been a submarine commander in the war (World War I) and had originally, as a German patriot, supported Hitler's policies. Now there was information through evangelical channels that he had been imprisoned in a labor concentration camp in Sachsenhausen. The general atmosphere in the country was one of growing discomfort and suspicion; but at the same time there was a good economy and the streets were safe.

A note by Klara in Brigitte's album: "Papa is on vacation! However, Brigitte occupies him more than his work ever can. It all starts in the mornings at 5:00 a.m. with a wrestling bout in bed.

Little Uli (Ulrich) is included. After that father and daughter decide, in loud whispers, where they'll go 'exploring.' And then the two set out, day after day, for their adventures. They'll dress in their oldest clothes, unless I catch them first. Then they go to the park and meet people and dogs, or look into pet stores, or buy a *Wurst* [sausage] in a bun on the street. Occasionally they graciously include Mutti and Uli in their wanderings."

I remember: It was a sunny, breezy day. I held Papa's right hand as we walked along the street. I didn't remember where we went, but I remembered the feeling of fun and adventure. When I suddenly had to "go," Papa held me over the curb.

Public restrooms must have been scarce in those days. I have talked with other people of my generation, who grew up in Europe, and they remember such scenes also. Men would sometimes urinate against a designated wall, in public, especially in France. I don't know what women did.

Written by Klara for her little girl on October 21, 1937:

"Once upon a time there was a little girl called Brigitte. During the day she was independent and quite a risk taker, even wild. But when it began to get dark, now that summer was over and fall came breezing in, the little girl crawled on her Mutti's lap and became quite gentle and affectionate. She wanted to hear soothing stories. Mother and daughter called this time of day *die blaue Stunde* [the blue hour]. The mother would read to her five-year-old girl or tell her tales of St. Martin or St. Nicholas or Christmas. And sometimes, when Brigitte was already in bed, but had a toothache or tummy ache, Mutti had to come and lie down with her to comfort her little girl."

"I borrowed a book," Klara continued her writing, "*Fröhliche Kinderstube* [*Happy Children's Room*], and from it I learned many games and verses. Now, when we have a rainy afternoon, we invite some neighbors' kids over—Jutta, Inge, and Ingetraud—and we have tea with all the dolls and the little doll cups and plates. Minna (the mother's helper) and I have real coffee and we all have tiny sandwiches. We also have a lot of fun making things with *Plastilin* [similar to Play-Doh]."

Brigitte had her first visit to the dentist in November 1937, at the age of five and a half. Mutti was scared that there'd be loud screaming, but Brigitte didn't fuss, even though she needed three fillings. (*There was no fluoridation of water at that time.*)

Here's how I remember it: I was scared of the dentist and the dentist's office, the chair, and especially the drill. It made horrible noises and it hurt. I didn't ever want to go to the dentist again!

On December 17, Klara took Brigitte and a friend, Inge Zaage, to their first theater experience. She reported: "The show was called *Hannchens Märchenträume* [*Little Hannah's Fairytale Dreams*] and produced in the *Haus der Arbeit* [House of Labor]. Both girls watched the play breathlessly and with total concentration, as Santa Claus, Little Red Riding Hood, the Wolf, and Puss in Boots paraded across the stage."

I remember this: I was looking at Inge in our apartment before we left for the theater. I was feeling jealous. Little Inge had a green velvet dress, much prettier than mine. And she had dimples. And she had her hair fixed with curls and a big bow. I felt that she was more loved and cherished than I was.

From the photo/life album: "The time of waiting for Christmas Eve was too much for Brigitte. On the afternoon of the twenty-fourth, she threw herself on the floor in front of the closed door of the living room, where Papa was trimming the tree, and screamed, 'I can't stand it anymore! I can't stand it anymore!' Fortunately, she calmed down enough to go to church with her parents and little brother. On the way home she asked, 'Papa, what do you like more, the church service or the presents?'

"Papa considered the question very seriously. Finally, he answered, 'The best thing is, first, the worship service and then the gifts.'"

In her own diary, Klara summarized the most important events for her of 1937.

"First of all, we're happy about our healthy kids. Brigitte is five and a half and Ulrich is one and a half. Uli's baptism was a high point this year and then my trip with Erich to Sonthofen. Kurt got his PhD and we all celebrated. Now he's also with Siemens in

Berlin. He has a girlfriend, Maria Tenzer. Tonight we'll celebrate *Sylvester* [New Year's Eve] with friends in the Ratskeller, as usual."

In February 1938, Klara took Brigitte for the physical examination, which was required before school registration. She was happy that her daughter passed with flying colors, including an intelligence test, although the results are not recorded. Now it was time to buy a *Ranzen* (school backpack) and other supplies. Little Gitte practiced writing her name in big capital letters on a slate board with a slate pencil. At this time Klara and Erich also considered her to be responsible enough to push her baby brother in his stroller outside on the sidewalk without direct supervision. That gave Klara some relief and time to write and read.

On the twenty-first of April 1938, Brigitte was enrolled in the Gutenberg Elementary School at age five years and ten months. As a good parent, Erich took a picture before they left home. Brigitte is standing in front of the apartment building. The new German flag, red with a white circle containing a black hooked cross, is seen behind her because the day before had been Hitler's forty-ninth birthday. (*On a side note, Hitler's favorite birthday present had been a model of the Volkswagen, designed by Ferdinand Porsche.*)

The flag's hooked cross, the swastika, had been adopted because of its ancient Aryan/Indian/Germanic history. The name derives from Sanskrit: *su* means "good," *asti* is "to be," and *ka* is a suffix. This symbol, more than three thousand years old, represents sun, power, and good luck. It is still used in a religious sense by Buddhists and Hindus. Interestingly, it was on the shoulder patches of the American Forty-Fifth Division in World War I and also used by the Finnish air force until after World War II.

Leaving for school, Brigitte is seen in the photo clutching an enormous cardboard cone in her right arm. All children who were starting school got one of these, filled with candy, fruit, and small items like pencils and coloring books. Brigitte is wearing the

Russian tunic-style dress that Klara had proudly made in a sewing class at the *Mutterschule* [Mothers' School].

On this first day of school, parents were welcomed with their child into the school and introduced to the middle-aged, gray-haired teacher, Fräulein (Miss) Teigschläger (*name changed by author*), who explained classroom procedures. Everyone was treated to a lovely recorder recital by some of the older students, followed by a brief invocation. From now on, the children would walk to and from the nearby school by themselves.

I remember: The school was ugly and old, built of purplish-red brick. The courtyard was just concrete, fenced in. Two swings, no slides. At recess, we played ball or skipped rope or drew squares on the ground and played hopscotch. I didn't like my teacher—she was so strict. One day she called on me and as I stood up, I was so scared that I peed in my pants. I was so embarrassed! One thing was good though—my hair was growing longer. Soon I'd be able to have braids.

When I was not in school I liked to play in the courtyard in back of the apartments. There was a boy next door who was fun to do stuff with. His name was Jürgen. One of us had to climb over the wall, which had colored pieces of glass sticking up on top. But we didn't have any problem with that. There was a plum tree in the corner and we snitched some and enjoyed them, and we often also played pretend games.

Klara wrote in the album: "Brigitte just lost her first baby tooth. Seems that it was just yesterday that she got this tooth. School vacation is July 15 to August 24. Papa, Brigitte, Uli, and I will spend most days on the beach, getting there by bicycle and ferry. Sometimes we'll go and enjoy our little plot in the *Schrebergarten* [victory garden] of Onkel Gutmann. The kids love to run around barefoot and dig in the soil and eat fresh fruit and veggies."

Erich's youngest brother, Helmut, was drafted into the navy at age nineteen and spent some time in Kiel while in officer training on a sailing ship, the *Schleswig Holstein* (named after the northern German province in which Kiel is located). He visited often, much admired by Gitte (Brigitte) and her little brother Uli (Ulrich).

One evening, over supper, he related a lesson in etiquette he'd had to endure that day at the noontime dinner:

"Today all of us were served a dessert. It was poached pear. But it turned out that those pears were still rather firm and quite slippery. Many of us tried to cut off a piece and then we were very embarrassed when it flew off the plate onto our lap or the table or the floor."

"How about yours?"

"Well, my pear had the same fate, and the other guys almost died laughing."

Another of Erich's brothers, Ernst, who worked as a physicist at Siemens in Berlin, married his sweetheart Christa. Later on, another brother, Ewald, also would work at Siemens and both of them later became directors of the company. Siemens was, and still is, a globally renowned manufacturing company of medical diagnostic equipment, electronic items, and other machinery. Erich's youngest sister, Ruth, called to say that she and her husband Heinrich had a baby boy, whom they named Uwe.

I remember this: I liked it when Papa and Onkel Helmut wore their uniforms. Papa's uniform had a long sword he wore at his side, with a gold tassel at the top. It was so impressive.

Erich apparently only wore a uniform on special occasions. It reminds me of the officers in the US Public Health Service, such as those working at the CDC (Centers for Disease Control and Prevention in Atlanta, Georgia), who also didn't always wear their uniforms, although now it is mandatory. My father had regular promotions in the civil service, but also had a navy ranking.

1938 was the year in which, by plebiscite (popular vote), Austria became annexed to the German Reich (*Östereich Anschluss*). In the United States, Hitler was *Time* magazine's Man of the Year. Also, the first Superman comic book was published. (*One such copy recently sold for one million dollars.*) In Saudi Arabia, King Abdulaziz had hired American engineers from Standard Oil of California to drill for water. After several years, they found not water, but oil. The king was not impressed and didn't come to see the well until a year later, when he arrived with a caravan of 440 automobiles to see what later turned out to be the largest supply of crude oil in the world.

There is no mention in my parents' papers of Kristallnacht, November 7, 1938, when in several cities in Germany, although apparently not in Kiel, Jewish stores and synagogues were damaged and Jewish people attacked and arrested. Perhaps my mother's birthday, November 7, overshadowed the news.

The next entry into Brigitte's photo/life album was written by Klara in September 1938. Reading it stopped me in my tracks. It is so poignant and sad in retrospect.

Klara wrote: "Yesterday, the 30th of September 1938, was a day of great joy and relief! With much anxiety we had all feared that a war might be imminent—then came the Munich Agreement and the great rescue of peace. I met for coffee with my neighbor, *Frau* [Mrs.] Zaage, early in the morning, at 7:00 a.m., to celebrate the good news!"

That was the meeting of England's prime minister, Neville Chamberlain, with Germany's president and chancellor, Adolf Hitler. Britain agreed that Germany could take back the Sudetenland, where the majority Germans had been poorly treated by the Czechs after World War I. Germans everywhere had been buying blue candles to raise money to help them. Hitler, on his part, promised peace. Chamberlain returned to London, saying, "I believe it is peace for our time."

Just a year later, World War II began when Hitler invaded Poland.

PART TWO

How Our Family Lived in Germany During the War Years

1939–1945

CHAPTER 8

1939: Kiel. World War II starts September 1, 1939. Early war experiences. 1940: Kiel and the move to Berlin.

Klara saved Brigitte's first report card: "April 1939. Brigitte is a lively student, who enjoys the schoolwork, comprehends new concepts quickly, and participates in the classroom with good understanding. Her work is satisfactory to good. Behavior is very good."

I remember how I felt. I loved to read my first book in school. It had colorful pictures of a beautiful yellow tabby cat. Her name was Muschi. I could already read the sentence "Muschi ist lieb" *[Muschi is nice]. I learned to read whole words, not phonics. That has made me a fast reader, even in other languages later, such as Latin, English, French, and recently Spanish.*

In the summer, the family visited relatives in Voerde and Düsseldorf again.

I have many black-and-white photos showing little Gitte at age seven and Uli at age three. I remember running around in the big backyard in Voerde with Uli, chasing chickens and climbing trees. In the kitchen, when I sidled up to my Oma, she would gently pinch my calf and call me "Mein lecker Beesken" *(my delicious little bite)—pronounced "mine lek-kah Beh-sken"—in Plattdeutsch (Low German), the dialect spoken in Voerde, which is quite similar to Dutch. That's understandable, since Holland is right across the Rhine.*

In mid-September 1939, Klara wrote a short, sad note in her own diary: "Our vacation time was clouded by fears of impending war. And now, as of September first, the war has befallen us. This is the second war in Erich's and my lifetime. Thank God the children have no idea of the difficulties of this time. Two days ago, we had an air-raid attack over Kiel by enemy planes. May we soon have victory and peace."

Germany invaded Poland and also occupied Czechoslovakia and regained control of Memel and Danzig. The Soviet Union was allied with Germany at this time and invaded Poland from the east. It also took control of the Baltic states of Estonia and Lithuania. There was a German-Soviet agreement on "spheres of influence," which was not discovered until 1945. Later in September, Hitler announced a great peace proposal and German families were much relieved at its possibility.

In Spain, after the civil war, Generalissimo Francisco Franco, another fascist leader, became head of state and was recognized by other nations. In Italy, Benito Mussolini, also a fascist, had made an alliance with Hitler as part of what was later called the Axis.

Brigitte, now a second grader, was promoted to using paper and pencil or pen, and she donated her slate board and pencil to her little brother, Uli.

I remember how excited I was when we were given a recorder in school. I came home and sat at the little table in the kitchen and showed it to Mutti. It was a wooden soprano recorder, made by Adler. During the next school year, I learned to play a few tunes, like "Schlaf, Kindchen, Schlaf" *(Sleep, Little One, Sleep),* "Freude, schöner Götterfunken" *(Ode to Joy—by Beethoven), and many folk songs. I kept that recorder for many decades and played folk tunes on it and Christmas carols. It was not until much, much later, in 1996, that I became more seriously interested in recorder playing.*

In November, according to Klara's notes, Gitte, age seven, told her parents that she was quite aware that there was no Santa Claus—that parents gave presents to their children. It was a bittersweet moment for Erich and Klara.

Erich's anticipated promotion to *Oberregierungsrat* (a higher civil-service grade) came through and with it a transfer to Berlin, the capital. He had to move on December 1, but the family had to wait until an apartment could be found. Klara and Erich felt sadness at the prospect of leaving Kiel. After nine years, they had made many friends and had become attached to the city and the blue Förde and the beaches. However, they looked forward to having a much larger apartment in Berlin and getting together with family members and friends who lived there.

From Brigitte's album, written by Klara during the Advent season:

Brigitte: Muttiiiiihh?!?

Klara: Yes, dear?

Brigitte: Mutti, I'm making you something for Christmas, but I can't tell you what.

Klara: Well, that's fine. Then it'll be a surprise.

Brigitte: I'm embroidering something for you, but I won't tell you what.

Klara: Well, I guess I'll have to be patient.

Brigitte: No, I won't tell you. I hope you can use it. Waltraud [the maid at that time] says that every mother can use a flower-pot coaster. I'm working on it all the time when you're not here and sometimes I even work on it at night in bed. I guess you're really, really curious, aren't you?

Klara: Terribly curious. But I guess I won't find out yet.

Brigitte: I won't tell you! What fun, isn't it, Mutti?

I remember going Christmas shopping with Mutti and Uli: it was a cold, gray day. We were going to a large department store that sounded like Voolvers. (In later years, I realized that's how I heard "Woolworth.") There were decorations and lights and it looked very festive. On the way to the big store, we passed by many lovely shop windows. Some had gold script and depictions of imported chocolates and little black Moors. I enjoyed looking at these, but of course I knew that there was no chocolate to be had inside. There were so many other beautiful advertisings, but the reality was that it was wartime and these things were not actually available.

I wonder now whether that early experience was the beginning of my lifelong skepticism in regard to all advertising and propaganda.

Klara's notes in my album from this time on have a tinge of sadness as she describes the wartime Christmas season. There was a shortage of coal, making it uncomfortably cold in people's homes in the evenings. Movie theaters and stores were unheated.

I remember that our bedrooms were unheated at night and how good it felt to crawl under the fluffy Federbett *(down comforter) and warm up. I learned to tuck the covers around my neck, covering my shoulders, and also under my feet, so that I slept in a cocoon.*

Klara had to learn to manage the new food-rationing coupons, and she glued some of them into the album. A coupon for rice, for instance, read: "375g Rice, N33/34, 18-12-39 to 14-1-40." (*That's less than one American pound and had to last for a month.*) There were coupons for bacon fat, oil or margarine, bread, and meat. Luxury items, like coffee, cigarettes, or chocolate, were almost unobtainable and soon a black market developed for these. For a while there were not even any potatoes to be had, even though they were the staple carbohydrate in the German diet (like rice in Asia and pasta in Italy).

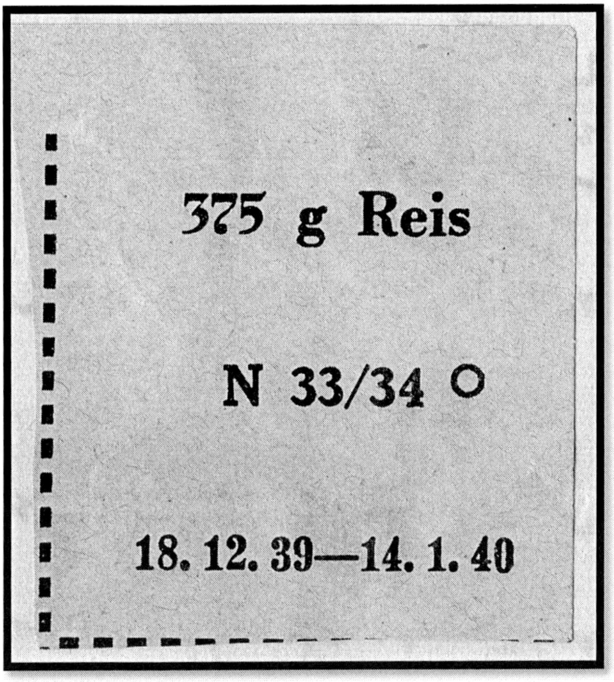

The worst part of this December of 1939 was that it was very lonely without Erich. Klara missed her husband and the children missed their papa. They had always been a close family. Adding to the gloom of cold, loneliness, and food shortages was the fact that the entire city of Kiel was now in blackout. Every evening, little Uli reminded his mother, "Mutti, time to pull the shades and drapes!" And only then did the little family sit down around the dining table, first to eat and then to read, paint with watercolors, do handicrafts, or play games. Uli once threw an assortment of toys on the table and said, "There, now it's a real family table!" Klara noted that a certain amount of clutter seemed necessary for happy family togetherness.

I have felt the same way throughout my life and perhaps that's why everyone feels comfortable in my home.

In Kiel, Gitte and Uli liked to play fantasy games. Gitte dressed up in her Mutti's old clothes and shoes, and Uli drove a toy truck noisily around and around under the table. Uli's bedtime was seven o'clock p.m. and Gitte's seven thirty p.m.

Everyone was very happy that Erich was able to come home and spend some time with the family over Christmas. There was a wonderful present for Klara—the piano she'd longed for. It was a pretty spinet in beautifully patterned chestnut wood. When opening the lid to expose the keyboard, one could read in gold script: Bogs & Voigt, Kaiserl. Oesterr. u. Koenigl. Span. Hoflieferanten [Bogs & Voigt, Imperial Austrian and Royal Spanish Court Suppliers] Musikhaus Kihr, Kiel—Falckstr. 21. Klara played by ear, forming chords to accompany folk songs, Christmas carols, and some other tunes. Erich tried his hand, also, and was able to play a little.

This piano made it through the war, although it became pockmarked by shrapnel. It eventually came to Atlanta, Georgia, United States of America, and now belongs to Eddy, my youngest son, and his family.

In January 1940, Erich had to return to Berlin. Finding an apartment for the family in the large and crowded capital city turned out to be difficult. Klara and the children had to stay on in Kiel. Both children caught whooping cough (*a common childhood disease at the time, though now it is rare because of the effective pertussis vaccine*). Brigitte also had two attacks of sharp, severe pain in the right kidney area.

I remember this well. Mutti took me to the doctor. I was sitting on the examining table and the doctor told me to take off my panties and lie down. She was quite pleasant, but I hated this! What was she going to do? She said, "Tut nicht weh; ist nur ein bisschen unangenehm." [Doesn't hurt; it's just a little unpleasant.]

The very fact that I remember the words and intonation verbatim shows how strong my emotion of fear was at that moment. The doctor probably catheterized me to obtain a clean urine sample. Apparently there was no definite diagnosis and the sharp pains eventually stopped.

A strange occurrence happened on May 10. Rudolf Hess, a close associate of Hitler's, flew a Messerschmitt Bf 110 fighter plane out of Augsburg to Dungavel, Scotland. He asked to speak to the Duke of Hamilton. Hess said that he'd come on a mission of peace and that Hitler had no wish to invade England and wanted to end the fighting. Hess's message was not believed and he was imprisoned.

Klara's next entry in Brigitte's album starts with a newspaper clipping of July 2, 1940, which she had saved and glued in. It is now very yellowed. (*I've translated it verbatim.*)

Englischer Luftangriff auf Kiel

Kiel, 2. Juli. In der Nacht vom 1. auf den 2. Juli 1940 führten im Schutze einer starken Wolkendecke nach Schleswig-Holstein eingeflogene englische- Flugzeuge einen Luftangriff von mehr als einstündiger Dauer auf die Kriegsmarinestadt Kiel durch. Wie immer bei derartigen Angriffen warf der Feind auch diesmal seine Bomben wahllos auf die Stadt, wobei er einige Treffer in der eng besiedelten Altstadt erzielte.

Er darf auch in diesem Falle den traurigen Mut für sich in Anspruch nehmen, durch seine Bombenabwürfe sowie durch Maschinengewehrfeuer auf friedliche Wohnungen neben dem Anrichten von Sachschaden mehrere Einwohner getötet oder verletzt zu haben, während auf das Industriegelände auf dem Ostufer abgeworfene Bomben lediglich Sachschäden anrichteten.

Der erfolgreichen deutschen Luftabwehr gelang es, von dem angreifenden Feind zwei Flugzeuge durch Flak abzuschießen.

English Air Attack on Kiel

During the night of July 1 to 2, English airplanes flew into Schleswig-Holstein. Under protection of a thick cloud cover, they attacked the *Kriegsmarine*

> [wartime navy] city of Kiel for over an hour. As usual, the enemy dropped bombs indiscriminately on the city, including several into the densely populated "old city."
>
> In this case again, the enemy can claim the sad responsibility to have caused, through bombing and through strafing with machine guns, not only damage to peaceful dwellings, but also several deaths and injuries to innocent citizens. In the meantime, the industrial areas toward the eastern shore sustained minimal damage. The German anti-aircraft defense was able to bring down two of the attacking planes.

By this time Germany had occupied Denmark and Norway to the north and Holland, Belgium and Luxembourg to the west. In early June, German troops had entered France. In "the miracle of Dunkirk," three hundred thousand fleeing British soldiers were evacuated from the harbor and beaches. On June 21, 1940, France surrendered. Hitler was now master of Europe. In England there was a new prime minister, Winston Churchill. He exhorted the British people to fight with "blood, toil, tears, and sweat". The war between Germany and England was primarily one of air raids bilaterally. It was the time of the *Blitzkrieg* [lightning war], including bombing of London and reciprocal attacks over German cities. At this time, in the United States, the Selective Service Act—the draft—had begun for men aged twenty-one to thirty-six. America, although officially "neutral," was actively assisting the Allies, especially Britain, with supplies and naval support.

The war didn't end soon, as Erich and Klara had hoped, and a Berlin apartment had not yet been found. However, the Buchmanns did have a pleasant interlude in August, when they enjoyed a vacation together in Malenta, the Holstein spa area. The kids had fun on the playgrounds and the adults hiked through the lovely landscape. Afterward Erich had to return to Berlin, and Klara,

Brigitte, and Ulrich to Kiel. Klara was becoming quite impatient about the delay in moving.

I have a memory of an episode at this time: Mutti had company, a lady with a baby and a little girl my age. I watched the mom take a bite of lunch, chew it, and then spit in on a spoon and feed it to her baby! The little girl came with me into our bedroom. She lay down on one bed and I was on the other one. We were supposed to take a nap, while Uli was sleeping on my parents' bed. The little girl lay on her back and showed me how to slide my feet up, bending my knees, and move my hips backward and forward. It made a nice feeling down below and came to a high point and then that made me relax. That afternoon was my introduction to "strained" baby food and to masturbation.

Finally, on the tenth of October, an apartment became available in Berlin and now the family could be reunited. Poor Klara then had to endure weeks of confusion, since a move in wartime was complicated. She had to go, on foot, to untold offices to register, obtain rationing coupons for food and other items, and scout out the area for shops. However, the whole family was happy with the spacious fifth-floor apartment, close to the Havel River, a lake, and woods. The disadvantage was that it was located rather far from the city's center. The address was Betckestrasse 7, Berlin-Spandau. Erich and Klara had a large master bedroom, and Brigitte and Ulrich each now had their own bedrooms. Brigitte was thrilled to help decorate hers with blue-painted walls. There was also a glassed-in sun-room, a large kitchen, a spacious dining room, and a living room. Brigitte was fascinated by a board on the wall of the hallway just outside the kitchen. Here, if someone in one of the rooms rang, a little tag would drop down with the name of the room. In this way the *Hausfrau* (woman of the house) could call someone in the kitchen to come and serve food or help in other ways.

I remember my room was narrow and long with a big window. I had a little teddy bear on my bed with the Steiff button in one ear. There were lots of books on my bookcase. My favorite book was Heidi, *by Johanna Spyri. I loved that story of Heidi and her grandfather on the mountain with all those goats and the wind whistling in the tall pine trees. But then Heidi is moved into the city by her aunt. She is supposed to be company for Klara, who can't walk and is in a wheelchair. Heidi is adventurous and entertains Klara, but she is also very homesick. Finally, she persuades Klara's father to let her visit her grandfather and let Klara go also. And up there on the mountain Klara eats fresh goat cheese and drinks milk and is encouraged to try walking, and she makes it! This book has wonderful pen-and-ink drawings, and I tried to imitate that style.*

I was glad Uli had his own room, too. Mutti made us both learn our new phone number: Siebenunddreissig-vierundsiebzig-nullfünf *(37-74-05). That number still reverberates in my mind, in German, rhythmically, after all these years.*

Klara met with her oldest childhood friend, Hilde, and another one, Lisbeth. That was a great joy. Slowly the family got used to the necessary means of transportation in the city: buses and streetcars. The Buchmanns, like most people, had no car. Although they had saved up for a Volkswagen, no one was able to buy a car during the war. But they managed to visit other Buchmann family members and got around very well. Fortunately, in their neighborhood there were also trails through the woods and pleasant riverside meadows for walks, play, and picnics.

Here are some of my Berlin memories:

I was in a new school now, a Lyzeum *(university prep school for girls; the equivalent for boys was* Gymnasium*). These big-city kids in school and everywhere in Berlin were so rude and fresh! They had the* "Berliner Schnauze" *(Berlin muzzle). I had to learn to talk and act like that, too. It took me quite a while to get to school and back every day. I had to walk about three blocks to the streetcar and ride about ten minutes on it, then walk another four blocks. That year, in third grade, I was taking German, geography, art, PE, and math.*

I really, really liked my math teacher—she was beautiful and smart. My best friend, Helga Spiess, liked her a lot, too. We tried to be like her. School started at eight in the morning and ran until one o'clock. We had a brief recess, when we could go out in the yard and have a snack and play some ball. Then when I got home we all had our midday dinner, Mutti, Hanna (our new mother's helper), Uli, and I. Papa ate his dinner in the cafeteria at his work. We had school on Saturday mornings, too, but Sundays were free.

What I didn't like was that the teachers now didn't say, "Good morning!" anymore; they said, "Heil Hitler." We had to raise our right arms and say it back. What was even worse was what happened when we had assembly. We had to keep our arm raised the whole time while we sang.

First we sang "Deutschland, Deutschland über Alles, über Alles in der Welt" *(Germany, Germany Above Everything, Above Everything in the World). The beautiful national anthem was based on lyrics written in 1841 by the liberal professor and poet August Heinrich Hoffmann von Fallersleben to encourage the many German provinces to unite into one Germany—not to become superior to other nations, but rather for Germany to become superior to the many individual principalities of the time. The famous melody is based on the slow movement of the Emperor*

Quartet by Franz Joseph Haydn. The anthem was adopted in 1922 by the Social Democratic President Friedrich Ebert and was retained by the Hitler regime.

Going on . . . Right after the anthem, we had to sing the "Horst Wessel Lied." *(Wessel was a leader in the SA, the Sturm Abteil or brown shirts, in the early days of Hitler's party.) That song begins,* "Die Fahne hoch, die Reihen fest geschlossen. SA marschiert . . ." *[The flag up high, the rows in tight formation. SA marches on . . .]. YOU should try to hold your arm up that long!*

Klara continued to write in Brigitte's album, and now she wrote in Ulrich's also.

"I tell the children bedtime stories every evening. The most popular these days is one with endless variations, about a thumb-sized little boy, *der kleine Däumling.*

In her daughter's album she wrote: "Brigitte is a very intelligent little girl, who loves school. She's not stubborn. She hasn't found a friend yet with whom she can play imaginative games, like she did in Kiel. In school she enjoys reading, writing, and anything in gym class, but standing in front of the class for a presentation is not one of her favorite things."

At the end of 1940, Erich and Klara, as usual, discussed some of the high points of the year. They talked about the discovery of the Rh factor in the blood in the United States. This promised to save many babies from being stillborn. They prayed that the war would soon be over. They hugged each other about being together again as a family in Berlin.

Klara wrote in her own diary, "I hope that my vagabond years and frequent changes of places to live are finally over. May Berlin give us roots and a steady environment, and may we soon have peace."

CHAPTER 9

1941: Wartime Berlin. USA enters war.
1942: Brigitte with scarlet fever, Erich with typhus.
Klara has a stillborn son.
Ice-skating. Sledding.

The early months of 1941 had surprisingly mild weather. By March, the Buchmanns had to turn on the heat only in the evenings. Another pleasant surprise was the absence during these months of English flyers on bombing missions.

However, on February 23, Erich and Klara received terrible news. Erich's youngest brother Helmut, a navy flier only twenty years old who had often visited them, was reported missing. He had been on a reconnaissance flight over the English Channel the night before. There was no report from the German navy of a plane shot down. Else, the older sister, who had helped raise Helmut in Voerde, listened to BBC (British Broadcasting Company) radio throughout the next days, carefully and secretly, but there was no report from the British side of a plane downed. We will never know what happened on that foggy night. Erich's mother, Mutter, couldn't ever quite recover from the loss of her youngest, handsome, cheerful, and promising child.

Why do we humans persist in sending our young men (and now also women) to war? Why can we not learn to channel our (largely testosterone-fueled) aggressions into other projects? Why is there not more funding and interest in this problem? Why are negotiation studies and peace studies not required curriculum in schools and universities? Why, instead of just military academies, do we not also support big, prestigious peace or negotiation academies?

I've sometimes wondered, jokingly, if it would be possible to put an anti-testosterone chemical into the water supply and make the world a better place! It might also cut down on overpopulation. But perhaps the best hope for saving humans and our planet is to have women become more powerful.

Erich was given his brother's personal items by the navy. Among them was his *Ahnenpass* (ancestor passport), a little booklet that he saved. As required for officer training, it listed his parents, grandparents, and great-grandparents, with dates of birth and marriage, place of birth, and religion, all duly stamped and signed by local clergy. (*I have that interesting* Ahnenpass *in my source material.*)

Summer in Berlin was as pleasant as it could be, considering that it was wartime. In the evenings, Erich liked to tell stories to his kids. Some of these revolved around *Klein Erna* (Little Erna). Little Erna stories featured a working-class Hamburg family and were written in the local dialect. Example: Mama leans out of the window and calls, "Klein Erna! Come in—time to wash your feet. Mama needs the bowl for the salad." Brigitte and Ulrich would dissolve in laughter.

"More, more!" they yelled.

"Okay," Papa continued, "here's another one: Klein Erna is playing with a cat. 'No, no,' cries her mama, leaning out of the window, 'don't pull her tail!' 'I'm not pulling it,' says Klein Erna, 'the kitty's pulling; I'm just holding on.'"

"One more," begged Gitte, and Papa agreed. "One day in school the teacher asks, 'Who can recite a nice poem?'

'I know one,' says Klein Erna.

> A fisherman sits on the Elbe's strand [the shore of the large river flowing into the Atlantic Ocean near Hamburg; it is affected by the tides],
> Holding a fishing pole in his hand.
> He wants to catch a bass,
> The water goes up to his knees.

"'That doesn't rhyme,' says the teacher.

"'Oh, yes, it does,' says Klein Erna, 'just wait 'til the tide comes in.'"

On June 18, Klara wrote in Brigitte's album: "We celebrated Papa's thirty-seventh birthday today. Brothers Ernst, Kurt, and Werner were able to come. We met in the Waldcafé, a *gemütliches* [cozy] coffee house in the woods. Brigitte demonstrated how she could braid her own hair now.

"The war is still on and there's no end in sight. With the loss of Helmut, it has hit our family hard. Werner has also been drafted and is in the air force. He has been in France and Spain."

I presume that my father was not drafted because of his research work.

Four weeks in July were spent on a *Kraft durch Freude* (strength through joy) vacation in the Sudetenland. This was a government-sponsored vacation program, offering very reasonable rates for working persons and their families. The start of the journey was strenuous. The Buchmanns had to get up at 3:00 a.m. to catch the train. It was very hot and crowded, but the family found a *Mutter und Kind* (mother and child) compartment. After arriving in Johannesbad, everyone had to hike up the mountain for over two hours to get to the inn.

I remember: Oh, I was so hot and so tired! Climbing and climbing and climbing and carrying my Rucksack *(backpack). I was so thirsty. Would we ever get to the top?*

Note that the current fashion of carrying water bottles was not in effect at that time.

The inn on top of the *Schwarzenberg* (Black Mountain) was lovely. Comfortable rooms, lounges, library, a game room with ping-pong tables. The best thing, considering that it was wartime, was the food, which was tasty and abundant. Everyone could eat all they wanted. The family-run inn provided Silesian specialties like dumplings with sauerkraut. Klara was delighted that real coffee (not *Ersatz,* a substitute) was served. The children met other kids and played in the pool. Adults did some serious hiking and mountain climbing in the *Riesengebirge* (Giant Mountains), drinking in the marvelous views of mountains and valleys, dotted with wooden houses typical of the region. In the last week, the blueberries became ripe and everyone had blue fingers and a blue mouth.

"We haven't been this tanned in a long time," wrote Klara. "We could almost forget the war, which has raged with violent cruelty on the eastern front during these weeks."

At this point, starting in August 1941, for no given reason, Klara stopped writing in her own album and diary. I don't know why. Perhaps the times had just become too painfully difficult. Klara didn't resume writing for herself until 1948. She did, however, keep up Brigitte's and Ulrich's albums.

In August 1941 Klara noted in her daughter's album, "Brigitte can now ride a bicycle." Later, she also pasted in a pencil-written note, which Brigitte had left on her Mutti's night table: "Dear Mutti, I wish you a good night. But I'm very sad, because I've got to wear those long, thick stockings." Klara added, "and I had been so happy to have found good, woolen stockings for the winter."

I remember this: I hated these stockings. They itched and itched and itched. I didn't like anything woolen, even if it kept me warm! I still loved to read. My favorite books at this time were stories of the American West by Karl May, like Winnetou, *and* Old Shatterhand. *(This German author had never visited America, but wrote enormously popular Westerns.)*

In December, at age nine, Brigitte started piano lessons, together with a little boy of the same age. Klara wrote that theory was also included, besides learning technique and some melodies.

I remember: Piano seemed like it should be fun. But I hated it when I practiced at home and made a mistake and Mutti made a noise, like "ugh." My teacher was also very picky. She concentrated on our mistakes and not on what we did well. It all made me nervous about playing when anyone was around.

Klara wrote that she tried hard to maintain a festive Advent atmosphere during this, the third wartime Christmas. Every evening there was some singing and piano and recorder playing at home, candles were lit and a window opened in the Advent calendar. Klara loved playing her beautiful piano, which she was able to play by ear. The piano stood in the large dining room. A painting of flowers hung on the wall above and a record player stood on a little table to the left. The family continued to use the dining room table as an evening gathering place. Although the children enjoyed themselves, Klara wistfully noted, "Will this finally be the last wartime Christmas?"

The war atmosphere had changed. Hitler had sent German troops into Russia, the treaty having been abandoned, expecting a quick victory with a *Blitzkrieg* (lightning war), as he had achieved with the other, now occupied, countries. Operation Barbarossa, which had been launched on June 22, 1941, was at first very successful, with the army advancing close to Moscow. But then, in December, bitter cold and snow and the Russian troops' counteroffensive stopped progress. The German forces were not receiving necessary supplies of food, fuel, or ammunition. Hitler had not even authorized warm clothing for his men because he had believed that the war would be over before winter! Just as it had happened to Napoleon's army 129 years before, the Russian winter defeated the invaders.

In addition, on December 7, Japanese aircraft attacked American ships in Pearl Harbor, Hawaii. Roosevelt and the US Congress declared war on Japan. Since Germany and Italy were Japan's allies, Hitler and Mussolini then declared war on the United States. Germany was now waging war in the East and also the West, with the large economic strength of the United States involved. In America, the only member of the US Congress voting against war was Jeannette Rankin (R) Montana. She had also voted against World War I. In Hawaii and California, the Japanese, citizens or not, were rounded up into "relocation camps," and many lost their livelihoods. Only recently has this tragic episode been more fully discussed.

In Germany, hundreds of communists, liberal critics of the government, and Protestant pastors, including Martin Niemoeller, had been incarcerated in concentration camps; and Jews, including those in Poland and the Soviet Union, as well as Romas (Gypsies) and homosexuals were also rounded up into the camps.

I've sometimes been asked whether my parents knew about the Holocaust. I don't think that they, their friends, and most other ordinary German citizens were aware of what was happening later in the Holocaust. I have no recollection whatsoever of hearing anyone talk about Jews in any context. The very fact that I later married a Jewish man attests to the fact that I was not exposed to any prejudice in my childhood. There is also no mention of anything about this in any of my parents' papers, albums, diaries, or letters, which I have in my possession. I've been asked whether I saw people wearing the yellow Star of David. I can honestly say that I don't recollect ever seeing anyone wearing it.

My parents did know that there were Arbeitslager *(work camps), where dissidents had been imprisoned. They had heard through the religious grapevine about certain Lutheran pastors who had been incarcerated because of their outspoken opposition to the regime. Erich and Klara were outraged and perplexed, but I can discern a fear of voicing their opinions too openly in their writings. When I asked my parents many years later about the Holocaust, they stated that they did not know about this at that time and I believe them. It has become commonplace to say that all Germans knew about it or should have known about it, but without a free press and with limited transportation available, without the internet, cell phones, and TV, how much would we ourselves know what goes on in another part of our country? It has also become commonplace to refer to all Germans as Nazis, but not all Germans, and not my parents, belonged to the NSDAP (National Socialist German Workers' Party), and not all Nazis were bad people.*

1942 came in with bitter cold. Klara noted that Brigitte had learned to make hot chocolate (with a chocolate substitute) herself and that her favorite Christmas present had been ice skates.

I remember: I loved to go skating. It was about a fifteen-minute walk to the Grimnitzsee *(a nearby lake), carrying my skates over my shoulder. When I got there, I put the metal sole of the skates under my shoes and tightened the little brackets on the sides with a key. And then I could glide around with the other kids, make turns, and have fun hopping over the little humps that formed when the lake froze! But later, when I went home, my toes really, really hurt. They were so cold; it was so painful! Why didn't I learn to stop before I got all frozen?*

My best friend now was Helga Spiess. We went to school together at the Ina Seidel School and did our homework and played together. We also were both registered as Jungmädel *(young girls), somewhat equivalent to Brownies in the United States and precursors of the* BDM (Bund deutscher Mädel, *the Association of German Girls), equivalent to Girl Scouts, but with political overtones. I loved the uniform: a brown, suede weskit jacket with four pockets and a dark skirt. Mutti had a hard time finding a used uniform for me. I now had long braids and I thought I looked pretty good, except that my legs were so skinny.*

I never did get into the real BDM because my parents disapproved of it. It featured more political content, like the Hitler Youth did for boys.

Klara continued evenings of reading and music during the cold winter. She played piano and everyone sang. Occasionally Brigitte joined in with her school-issued recorder, which she loved. Favorite evening songs were *"Der Mond ist aufgegangen"* (The Moon Has Risen) and *"Kein schöner Land in dieser Zeit"* (No Land More Beautiful in this Time). Erich continued tales of Klein Erna.

"This story is called 'Piety.' Uncle Emil died and was cremated. Mama, Klein Erna, and Aunt Frieda are taking the urn with the ashes to the cemetery. Every sidewalk is pure ice. Aunt Frieda keeps slipping and falling down. After she falls down for the third time, she opens the urn and says to Klein Erna and Mama, 'Enough with the piety; now I'm going to use the ashes.'"

From my own memory: It was springtime and we were on vacation at the Heidehof *(Heather Inn). What I liked most were the animals. Uli and I were allowed to handle the baby chicks and rabbits. I fell in love with the black rabbit, Langohr (Long Ear). I held him up against my chest and stroked his soft fur and put my cheek on his head and he liked it. I learned what rabbits really love to eat: plantain, dandelions, and clover, and I picked those fresh greens for my favorite bunny. Oh, how I wished I could keep this rabbit and take it home! But I knew it was not possible. There were many things one wished for that were not possible.*

On the way home, while still on the train, Brigitte developed a severe sore throat and fever. The next day, when a rash appeared, she was diagnosed as having scarlet fever.

This streptococcal infection is easily treated with penicillin today, but that was not available in 1942.

Brigitte was observed closely and did develop a slight case of glomerulonephritis, a kidney complication, but fortunately not the other dreaded complication, rheumatic heart disease. She recovered completely.

I remember this very well: What a sore throat I had! I tried to eat a bite of sandwich on the train home, and it scratched my throat something awful when I swallowed. At home I was put in quarantine. I had to stay in my room for six weeks! Couldn't play with Uli or my girlfriends. Couldn't go to school. On our common birthday on June 30, Uli had his celebration in the living room and I had mine in my bedroom. But it was still a good day. I was ten and Uli was six. Poor Mutti—she had to shuttle back and forth. When she came into my room to take care of me, she put on a white lab coat that hung on the door. And then when she left, she hung it up and washed her hands. She also had to take care of Papa for a while, but then he had to be hospitalized in the navy Olympia Lazarett (a hospital and recovery center).

Erich had developed a severe infectious disease, typhus, with a draining abscess on his chest. He was very ill and it took a full eight weeks for him to make a complete recovery.

During this time, Klara was pregnant. Early in September, at seven months, she no longer felt the baby moving. She called Mutter (Erich's mother), who had a lot of experience after having fifteen children. Mutter said not to worry yet. However, one evening two weeks later, Klara began to have cramps and severe bleeding. She called an ambulance. The city was in blackout and the ambulance drove without lights. The driver wanted Klara to sit in the rear, but there was a sickening odor in there and Klara could not tolerate it. She could not see anything in the dark, but insisted on climbing in with the driver in front.

"What's causing that dreadful stench?" she asked.

"I'm afraid that's blood and maybe even body parts," he answered. "With all the air raids and so many wounded and killed, we don't have time to clean." With the "ta-doo, ta-doo" siren squealing, Klara—feeling scared, hemorrhaging, and in a lot of pain—finally reached the hospital. She had to go through labor and sadly delivered a stillborn, perfectly formed baby boy. The cause of death was never established. Klara had lost a lot of blood and had been close to death.

The summer of 1942 in Berlin had proved to be terrible. First, Brigitte had scarlet fever, then Erich came down with typhus, and finally Klara suffered a premature delivery of a stillborn baby. In addition to the illnesses, there were the ever-present air raids, the food and clothing shortages, and the very bad news from the Eastern Front, where thousands of young men were dying at Stalingrad and elsewhere in the Soviet Union.

In Africa, General Erwin Rommel, the "Desert Fox," had progressed to El Alamein, ninety-six kilometers west of Alexandria, Egypt. Alexandria was the home of the Nahmias family, whose youngest son, André, was a teenager. (*He was to become my husband fourteen years later, when we met in medical school in Washington, DC!*)

Rommel was an innovative *Panzer* (tank) commander, who was liked by the Hitler regime because of his successes and by the Arabs because they considered him a liberator from the British. However, Rommel did not receive the supplies he requested from Germany, where attention was focused on the Eastern Front. The British forces under General Montgomery, whose troops and equipment vastly outnumbered Rommel's, finally defeated him at Alamein. The legend of the Desert Fox lived on, however. He was much admired on all sides, not only for his clever tactics, but also for his humanitarian spirit.

When Rommel returned to Berlin, he tried to convince Hitler of the impossibility of winning the war in Africa. He was not successful in this and was reassigned to the Western Front, where he was later wounded. By June 1944, after the landing of Allied forces in France, he was convinced that the entire war was hopelessly lost and that Hitler must be stopped. This opinion could not be tolerated by the regime, and in October he was secretly arrested. He was given the choice of execution as a traitor or suicide. Rommel chose suicide by poison. He was buried with full military honors, and the German people did not learn of his opposition to Hitler's policies or his arrest.

In Germany and elsewhere, Jews were still being rounded up. Now recognizing the crisis situation, many tried desperately to leave, but few other countries reached out to help. In the United States, the *Christian Century* warned its readers not to succumb to

Jewish propaganda and not to believe the alleged German misdeeds. Roosevelt did not help Jews to immigrate into the United States.

The American Lutheran pastor Reinhold Niebuhr preached and also broadcast on the *Voice of America* against the persecution of Jews in Germany. Niebuhr had many relatives in Germany, some also famous ministers. He was also the author of the well-known Serenity Prayer: "God, give us the grace to accept with serenity the things that cannot be changed, courage to change the things that should be changed, and wisdom to distinguish the one from the other." It seems to me to be based on the Anglican Book of Common Prayer: "O Lord we beseech thee mercifully to receive the prayers of thy people which call upon thee, and grant that they may both perceive and know what things they ought to do, and also may have grace and power faithfully to fulfill the same." That's not surprising, since Niebuhr's wife was British and Anglican. The Serenity Prayer was later adopted by the twelve-step programs.

I remember: It was late fall and Mutti went off on her bicycle to some farms about half an hour away to get some Rüben *(turnips) and also some greens to decorate the apartment for Advent. Papa had come back the day before from a trip to Denmark with a delicious ham and some butter. We were going to have a fantastic dinner!*

I was playing outdoors as much as possible. I roller-skated on the sidewalk or played with a top that I could spin with a string. In the courtyard, I threw a big, soft ball against the brick wall, counting. One—I just threw it against the wall and then caught it. Two—I pushed it around behind my back and then against the wall, first to left and then to the right, and then caught it. Three—I pushed the ball under each knee and then against the wall. Four—I threw the ball, turned myself around, and caught it. And so on.

Indoors I played Mühle *(Mill) and* Mensch ärgere dich nicht *("Man, don't get mad," roughly equivalent to Trouble) and chess with Helga or Uli or Mutti or Papa. I was also playing some Christmas carols by ear on my recorder. The day before, our family and the Groth family had gone to the opera together to see* Hänsel und Gretel *by Engelbert*

Humperdinck. I didn't really like it. Something about it, perhaps the music, made me feel uncomfortable. It was not as I expected, since I liked the fairy tale.

My last report card had caused an uproar at home. The grades were fine, but the teacher had written a comment: "Brigitte has a tendency to talk in class and not pay attention." Well, I did get bored when the pace was slow. Usually I just doodled, but sometimes I started to whisper to a classmate.

*I felt that I learned a lot from just reading at home. Mutti and Papa let me take any book I wanted out of the bookcase. I read all the fairy tales that the brothers Grimm collected and wrote down in their travels through Germany and surrounding areas. Those tales were interesting and fun, with everything from heroes, princesses, fairies, witches, monsters, and good people and animals, as well as sneaky ones. One tale was "*Hänsel und Gretel*" who got sent into the woods by a mean stepmother. The first two times, they dropped pebbles and found their way home, but the third time they dropped bread crumbs, which were eaten by the birds. So now Hänsel and Gretel were lost. They wandered around and found a hut, covered with gingerbread and candy, where they were caught by a wicked witch who planned to fatten them and then eat them. But luckily they escaped and the witch got burned up in the oven. I also liked "*Schneewittchen*" (Snow White), who ran away from her jealous stepmother and was helped by the seven dwarfs, and "*Rumpelstilzchen*" (Rumpelstiltskin), who helped a beautiful maiden spin gold from straw, but demanded her firstborn child later unless she could guess his name. She did guess it. There were many, many more stories. It was a very big book. I guessed these were all stories people told each other on long winter nights. I still have this book.*

Much later, when I read and watched the Disney versions of these fairy tales, I was appalled at how they had been changed. It's as if these powerful tales had been dipped in sugary icing!

Going on with my recollections: I was also reading Hans Christian Andersen's fairy tales. He was a Danish writer. I didn't like these stories so much. They seemed depressing, especially "The Little Match Girl," who stood at a street corner, cold and hungry, selling matches, and finally froze to death. Even "The Little Mermaid" and "The Ugly Duckling" seemed sort of whiny stories to me.

I read some of Shakespeare's plays and thought they were terrific. The storylines were fun and the dialogue was so realistic. The other book I liked was *Vom Winde verweht (Gone with the Wind)* by Margaret Mitchell. I really liked the main character, Scarlett O'Hara. She seemed big and strong and sturdy to me. Of course, I read all these books in German. Shakespeare translated into modern German is a lot easier to read than the old-fashioned version that was compulsory reading in high school later in America. Another surprise for me was, years later, seeing the movie *Gone with the Wind.* I was disappointed to see Scarlett played by Vivian Leigh, a tiny, dark-haired, and soft-spoken British actress.

I also remember this, a life-changing event for me: I was reading a book called *Am Puls des Lebens (On the Pulse of Life).* It was written by a doctor who told little vignettes about his patients. He described how a thyroid hormone deficiency could make someone sluggish and fat, while an excess of thyroid hormone could make someone nervous, thin, and bug-eyed. He wrote about lung diseases, like tuberculosis, which could waste a patient away, and about heart failure, which could cause shortness of breath and swelling of the ankles. The author's stories were like little mysteries, and the diagnoses and cures were thrilling. This book was so fascinating to me that I determined that I would become a doctor. That determination never faded, and I did become a physician.

Hurray—it snowed and I could go sledding! I had a red sled made of wooden slats with metal runners. There was a steep hill in the woods nearby where we kids all would go. Hurray! Now I was zipping downhill, sitting on my sled, and steering by sticking out my feet and touching the ground lightly on either the right or the left. Once we were down, we had to pull the sled back up by a rope. I'd gone down many, many times and it was getting late. But just one more! I zoomed down—I lost control—I crashed into a tree trunk! Ouch! My chin had smashed into the tree and I was bleeding. I actually got a hole in my cheek below my mouth on the right. I could stick my tongue through it!

I still have a little scar there, but I don't remember anything else about it. I didn't see a doctor and it certainly didn't diminish my joy in sledding or speeding or risk taking.

Christmas 1942 was, again, a brief interval of greens, songs, candlelight, and a few gifts and sweets in the midst of a cold, gray, generally deprived wartime winter.

I remember these moments: It was Christmas Eve day. Mutti sent me out to buy some milk, bread, and cheese. I went out bundled up. We hadn't seen the sun in weeks. It was bitterly cold and windy. At the store, I had to stand in line for a long time and tried to keep my hands from freezing. Finally, I got up front and the saleslady filled up my blue-speckled enamel pitcher, which I'd brought with me. She gave me skim milk, thin and bluish. Bread and cheese were not available. Somehow I didn't mind the gloom, though, because I knew that night would be Christmas Eve.

On Christmas Day, I was reading my favorite present, a new book. Company arrived for a visit, but I kept on reading. Mutti got very mad at me and said I was unsociable. Later in the day, she made Uli and me write thank-you notes. She looked at mine and said, "Can't you write nicer notes? Yours are so stiff." Mutti scared me sometimes, because I never knew when she'd be nice and when she'd be mean. She sometimes acted as if she didn't really like me at all. It was unpredictable, so in general I tried not to make waves or stand out. I admired people, especially heroines in my books, who were exuberant and brave and attention getting, because I couldn't act like that myself.

At year's end, Klara wrote in Brigitte's album, "We're grateful that Erich and I overcame serious illnesses. Both of us came close to death, and we're glad that the children still have their parents."

CHAPTER 10

1943: War raging. Daily air raids.
Evacuation from Berlin to Voerde. Country life.
1944: War worsens. Werner killed.
Many German cities under heavy air-raid attacks.
An enemy fighter plane attacks our train station. Back briefly to Berlin.

March 1943 brought severe and frequent bombings. Night after night, the Buchmann family woke to the siren's wavering howl, wearily got up, dressed, and trudged down six flights into the air raid shelter.

I remember these feelings: I hated to hear the siren and to have to get up in the middle of the night. I hated to put on those scratchy woolen stockings. I hated to carry my suitcase down. I was sleepy and scared.

During an alarm, we couldn't take the elevator and had to walk down and up. But since we children always walked in the daytime, too, climbing five flights routinely from street level to our apartment didn't ever bother us.

It was so hard to sit there in the basement with all our sleepy neighbors and crying babies and scared faces. There was a young woman who was pregnant, and I heard Mutti whisper with other neighbors that this lady had diabetes and was in a precarious state. I kept looking at her large tummy and wondering what was going to happen.

Mutti always carried our photo albums in her suitcase and Papa carried important papers and an extra change of clothes for us, as well as some snacks. It was cold in the shelter and we never knew how long an air raid would last. We also never knew what we'd find when the end-of-alarm siren finally blew its long, steady tone. Would we still have a home? Or was everything gone and destroyed? This uncertainty flavored our nights and days. I tried to shut such thoughts out of my mind.

The continuing destruction of Berlin was a daily horror and the news from many other cities was equally bad. Klara's aunt and uncle in *Köln* (Cologne) were bombed out, their home blasted out in an instant one night. Gone were their lovingly selected antiques, which they had polished regularly with respect and care, their many collected books, and their well-tended plants. Their photos were burned, and so were their beds, chairs, tables, and all their other furniture. Gone was their Meissen porcelain, and the silver and crystal inherited from their families. Everything was burned to ashes in one night. Gone their comfort, security, and so many memories—their whole previous lives. At least they themselves survived.

The terrible losses in the Soviet Union also weighed heavily on every citizen's mind. In February, the German army, starving and freezing, had surrendered to the Russians. Ninety-one thousand men were sent to Siberia. Only one in twenty would survive. Some men did not return to Germany until ten years later! A large number of this generation of young men had been lost.

Klara and Erich tried to keep the children's emotional and spiritual environment as normal as possible. The war was not discussed in the children's presence.

I remember some scenes of Easter of that year, 1943: We were in church and as I heard the story of the passion of Christ, his suffering and death and the final glory of his resurrection, I was moved to tears. The Bach chorale "O Haupt voll Blut und Wunden" *(O Sacred Head Sore Wounded) reverberated in my mind for weeks and made me sad and contemplative. After church, our whole family spent the afternoon hiking in the springtime woods, enjoying the resurrection of nature. I loved springtime. The other day I put on a summery dress, even though it was still pretty cold, and ran along the street singing, "I'm springtime!"*

I had a new friend, Günther. He was two years older than I and taller, and he was great to play with. He promised me that after the war would be over, he'd take me in his father's U Boot *(submarine) to Africa and buy me an elephant.*

Klara wrote in her diary, "Our feeling of security is gone. Oh, if only this sorrowful wartime were over. We try hard to shield the kids from the worst news."

Göbbels gave a speech on the radio, acknowledging that catastrophic defeat was possible. He roused the population to *"Totalkrieg"* (total war) and called for national mobilization of all factories. Like Churchill in England, he worked to keep up hope and resistance in the population.

Erich was sent on a trip to France and when he returned, he told us an interesting experience he'd had. He visited someone who had been a prisoner of war in World War I and assigned to work for Erich's father in the dairy and mill in Voerde. The Buchmann family and the French POW became good friends and now Erich looked him up. Even though Germany was occupying France, Erich was welcomed by the whole family and had a heartwarming time with them.

I remember: Summer vacation was fun! Every day seemed like Sunday. We went to the beach on the Havel River and to the lake, and we picked raspberries. In our apartment complex there was a huge sandbox, where I went with my brother, Uli, and met friends. We built castles and farms and made up stories about knights and princesses.

On rainy days, my best friend Helga came over often and we played with the big dollhouse Papa had built for me the previous Christmas. It had two stories and six rooms. My little girl doll was called Ursula. She wore a blue dress and liked to go on the roof at night and take moonbaths. Helga's doll was Gisela, in a red dress. She took sunbaths.

Another game we played went like this: One kid put his fist on the table with the thumb sticking up. The next kid put his fist around the thumb and had his own thumb sticking up. We went on doing this while we moved our hands in a circle and chanted this ditty: "Wir fahren nach Amerika und wer fährt mit?" [We're going to America and who comes along?] At this point the next hand was added. Then we went on, "Die Katze mit dem langen Schwanz und die fährt mit!" [The kitty with the long, long tail and she comes along!] And here the next fist went on, until the "long, long tail" collapsed. Never did it enter my mind that I might actually go to America someday.

One day, as I was playing with Uli outdoors, some kids came running, excited. "Come and see—we're gonna show you something!" We crossed the street and ran into the courtyard of another apartment complex. There was something about this that didn't feel quite right—the kids were acting as if they knew they were doing something wrong, and yet, of course, we ran with them. We climbed up a few flights of stairs and the kids showed us an apartment, which was still furnished, but seemed empty. The doors were open. "Eine Zigeuner Wohnumg" *(a gypsy home), the kids whispered. We didn't enter and left.*

I don't remember ever hearing any more information, but in retrospect I wonder, of course, whether the people who lived there were arrested.

Klara wrote an article on children's safety in the home, to be published in a women's magazine. A photographer came to the apartment and took pictures of Brigitte and Ulrich opening the door to a stranger. Klara's article warned against this and many other dangers, like leaving panhandles on the stove within a child's reach.

Like so much else in a time of violence and war, this is somewhat ironic when every night there were children killed in bombing attacks.

My remembrance: Food was getting ever more scarce. One day I was sitting in the kitchen with Uli, and Mutti was serving lunch. We kids both had made a mound of the mashed potatoes on our plates and another mound of the Grünkohl *(kale). There was no meat, of course. Then Mutti dribbled a little bacon fat into the craters we'd dug in our two mounds.*

Bacon fat must have been a rare treat indeed for me to remember that scene so vividly. I even remember the smell of the kale and bacon. I was very skinny as a child and even as a teenager.

I also remember how Papa could be so funny. All the time he was quoting something from Wilhelm Busch. In the mornings he said, "Guten Morgen, guten Morgen, haben sie was zu besorgen? Tabak, Pfeife, Fidibus, alles was man haben muss" (Good morning, good morning, do you need anything? Tobacco, pipe, lighter, everything one needs).

The wonderful rhythm of it has stuck with me to this day. Wilhelm Busch (1832–1908) wrote and drew what we would now call comics. His most famous one was Max und Moritz, *published 1866, about two little rascals who get into one mischief after another. The American strip,* Katzenjammer Kids, *seems to me to have been based on this. I still have a large, tan, pigskin-bound, coffee-table book of Busch's works, and it's a delight to read through the different "comics," like* "Hans Huckebein, der Unglücksrabe" *(Hans Bent-leg, the Unlucky Raven) and* "Die fromme Helene" *(The Pious Helen). The illustrations are pen and ink, drawn by Busch himself, and they catch your attention. When I read Dr. Seuss stories to my grandchildren now, I'm strongly reminded of Busch's work, and I wonder why he hasn't received more recognition.*

A shocking event happened in July: Erich and Klara had made family reservations for a short vacation in the *Lüneburger Heide* (the heath and heather area of Germany). A few minutes before leaving home, when everyone was all dressed and packed and standing in the hallway, ready to leave, there was a phone call. The innkeeper called to say that the hotel was completely filled with refugees from a recent heavy firebombing attack on Hamburg!

A book about this horrific air attack was translated into English in 2006 by Joel Agee: Der Untergang (The End: Hamburg 1943 *by Hans Erich Nossack, a well-known German writer, who lived in Hamburg at that time). He was vacationing on the other side of the Elbe River and witnessed the fearful events. On July 27 and 28, 1943, the RAF (Royal Air Force) repeatedly bombed Hamburg, at one time utilizing eighteen hundred planes! The resulting firestorm destroyed more than half of the city, killed over forty-five thousand people, and created more than a million refugees.*

Reading about it made me wonder again about the military commanders who ordered the bombing of civilians and their homes. Surely it must already have been evident by then that civilians in a war cannot (in Germany) or will not (in England) rise up and overturn their government. They just endure.

To my mind, it is truly reprehensible to order such barbaric slaughter. I also consider it unethical to follow an order to do so. It's all the more disturbing that the pilots, who flew over cities and dropped their bombs, didn't even see the torn-apart or burned bodies of the mothers and children they had just killed or the destruction and fires of their homes. The recent book Among the Dead Cities: The History and Moral Legacy of the WWII Bombing of Civilians in Germany and Japan, *by A. C. Grayling, a respected British philosopher at the University of London, discusses the moral and practical aspects of these events. I am glad that the bombing of civilians is now considered a war crime, just like killing civilians in concentration camps or dislocating populations and causing them to be refugees with many dying of famine and disease. However, unfortunately, such practices still continue in the world of today.*

As I was revising this manuscript early in 2010, the United States was involved in two wars. The invasion of Iraq was begun in 2003 and featured a "shock and awe" bombardment of Baghdad, which we could vividly observe on television. The flaming city and the destruction brought up painful childhood memories in me that I thought I had permanently suppressed. The war in Afghanistan, despite military attempts to limit "collateral damage," still results in civilian casualties. "Collateral damage"—I sneer at that obfuscating, neutral-sounding term for murder. Murder of children, women, and men, who are civilians. At least the press is now using the term "civilians killed" and the military apologizes when it happens.

Two days after the bombing of Hamburg, the Buchmann family had made different travel plans. They took the train to

Voerde to have a whiff of country air and to see the relatives. There they had a good time, expecting to be there for eight to ten days.

Then came the shocking news: an evacuation order for all women and children from Berlin. Klara saved the newspaper headline and article in Brigitte's album. *I have translated it here:*

Berliner! Berlinerinnen!

Der Feind setzt den Luftterror gegen die deutsche Zivilbevölkerung rücksichtslos fort. Es ist dringend erwünscht und liegt im Interesse jedes Einzelnen, der nicht aus beruflichen oder sonstigen Gründen zum Verbleiben in Berlin verpflichtet ist (Frauen, Kinder, Pensionäre, Rentner usw.), sich in weniger luftgefährdete Gebiete zu begeben.

Berliner! Berlinerinnen!

The enemy continues his air raid terror against the German civilian population without consideration for women and children. It is highly recommended that everyone who is not required to stay in Berlin for work, professional, or other reasons, immediately evacuate into areas with less danger from the air. This applies particularly to women, children and retirees.

Mutter (Erich's mother and "Oma" to the children) offered to let Klara and the children stay on in her house in Voerde. They could use a large corner room. Erich had to return to work in Berlin.

I remember it so well: I loved it in Voerde! The backyard was huge. I could climb up the plum trees and the pear trees and eat the fruit still warm from the sun. Every so often we heard the train go by; it ran right behind the back fence.

There was a chicken coop and I was allowed to collect the eggs. The hens made a funny, excited, and proud sound when they'd laid an egg, "googooGOOgoogoogoogoo." One Sunday I saw how Oma caught a chicken for dinner. She held its head and put its neck on a tree stump and then hacked the head off with an ax. After that, the chicken still ran around for a little while, without a head! Then Oma held the chicken upside down to drain out the blood and took it into the kitchen, where it was plunged into a big pot with boiling water. After the water had cooled a bit, I was detailed to pluck the feathers. That was not an easy job! After that, we singed the remaining stubble with a candle, causing a vile odor. Then Oma cooked the chicken. She made soup and also separated some meat for the main course at noontime dinner.

I admired Oma. She had fifteen children and seemed to be able to do everything. And she did it calmly and competently. I can still always picture her in my mind, standing in her large kitchen, holding a round loaf of home-baked, crusty bread against her chest and slicing it with a big, sharp knife—from the outside toward her chest!

Papa called from Berlin when the phone lines were open. He could no longer live in our apartment anymore either. It was too dangerous. I didn't know exactly where he was in Berlin. The scientists were in a secret place. He did secret research. It had something to do with underwater explosions and protecting ships from torpedoes. He told me that they could make the ship in the shape of a wave and that helped. He told me to keep it a secret and I was doing that, but I thought he was probably joking. Still, you never knew. Mutti and Papa listened to the BBC on the radio and that was truly a very deep secret.

In November 1943, Klara wrote in Brigitte's album, "Berlin is largely a wasteland due to the bombs; our family is separated; we don't know when we will be reunited. I sorely miss my own home."

Not until reading and translating these notes by my mother did I become aware of how very difficult this time as an evacuee had been for her. She had to adjust from living in a spacious apartment in Berlin, with relatives and friends nearby, to making do with two children in one room in her mother-in-law's house in the country for an indeterminate time period. In front of us, she kept up her spirits, while we children were thoroughly enjoying our time in the country.

I remember more about this time: Outside the kitchen door was the doghouse and a big, white dog, who was chained. His name was Möwi and he was not all that friendly. One day he bit my brother Uli on the arm. Uli was really afraid of dogs after that and I couldn't blame him. A little farther down from the doghouse there was a stable for two sheep. The spring lambs were growing up now. They'd been so cute and soft and white earlier in the year. I loved holding them in my arms sometimes. Then there was a cat that lived in this stable also. She was black and white and very affectionate. She rubbed around my legs and purred.

When we were outdoors, we wore Klumpen *(clogs). They were made out of wood and looked just like the ones the Dutch people wore. When we entered the house again, we left them at the door and walked around in our socks. The* Plattdeutsch *(Low German) dialect spoken by the country people here was very similar to Dutch also. Of course, Holland was just across the Rhine river.*

In the backyard, there was a metal bar attached to two trees. I loved to hang from it and turn upside down. There also was a clothesline. Every so often I saw some narrow, oval-shaped, cotton-knit items of underwear hanging there. But when I asked what they were, no one would tell me.

School started and we were still in Voerde. I was going to the Oberschule *(middle school) in Wesel. Uli went to the one-room elementary school in Voerde, where Papa also had gone as a child. Every morning I walked half an hour to the Voerde train station. Mostly I didn't mind. I looked at the dew-glimmering fields in the cool morning mist and at the cows. There were a lot of dairy cows here, black-and-white Holsteins. They were quite tame and came to the fence and let me pat them on the nose. They could stick their tongues way up into their nostrils.*

The train took about fifteen minutes. In the train station in Wesel, there were big posters on the walls. One was a black silhouette of a man in profile with his finger to his mouth. On top of the poster it said, "Psst! Der Feind hört mit" (Psst! The enemy is listening). Another poster read, "Räder müssen rollen für den Sieg" (Our wheels are rolling for victory). I didn't pay much attention; I knew it was all propaganda. Just like ads in the stores and news on the radio and in the newspapers. Many years later, I heard about some American slogans of the time: "Loose lips sink ships" and "a slip of the lip may sink a ship."

It was a ten-minute walk in the town of Wesel to the school, a pretty, yellow-brick building. But I didn't feel welcomed here. Everyone else had been together for years and they didn't seem to want to accept a stranger. Well, I just had to do the best I could. My favorite subject at that time was Latin. "Amo, amas, amat, amamus, amatis, amant" (I love, you love, he/she/it loves, we love, you love, they love).

Twelve years after the war, I visited Wesel. I remembered the direction I used to walk to school, but nothing looked familiar. Then I found out that after we had left the area, the entire town had been bombed into ruins and all the buildings I now saw were new.

Continuing my remembrances: After school, it was a walk to the train station again, the ride, and then the walk home. Sometimes I got off at the station just before Voerde and then walked along the tracks, just for a change. I observed and admired the wildflowers along the tracks. They were so beautiful and so strong. Every few weeks, a new batch started to bloom. I have loved wildflowers ("weeds" to some people) ever since. All the time I was walking, I listened for the distant rumble of the train, of course. Often I'd pick a little bouquet to bring home. On the days I rode the train farther to the Voerde station and walked home on the street, with pastures on both sides, I saw the dairy cows again. At this time of day, they were lying in the shade under trees and they were chewing their cud. It looked very relaxing.

Although I only lived in Voerde for a year and a half, this experience influenced me disproportionally for the rest of my life. Seeing country life, where people were close to nature and acted in a matter-of-fact manner about raising crops and animals, harvesting, butchering pigs, chickens, and lambs, and preparing food from them has made me more realistic. Observing my capable and calm Oma helped me to cope later in life when I was working with patients in my medical profession and simultaneously raising three children, cooperating with my husband in entertaining and traveling, and managing house, maid, pets, and yard. When I was nursing one of my babies while reading the paper or a medical journal or watching TV, I often remembered my Oma and thought about how she had given life and nourishment to so many children.

At Christmastime 1943, Klara wrote some comments into Brigitte's album. "Long days and nights lie behind us this year. There's the constant homesickness for my own home and neighborhood, which I so painfully miss in a thousand daily details. There's the worry about our Papa in Berlin and about our lovely household. There are the long days after an air-raid attack before we receive word about our loved ones in Berlin and our apartment. There are the endless hours at night from the first radio announcement, 'Achtung! Achtung! Mitteilung an Alle. Feindliche Flieger über Aachen . . .' [Attention! Attention! Public Announcement. Enemy flyers over Aachen . . .], telling us that bombers are on the way toward Berlin, until the *'Rückflüge aus Mitteldeutschland'* [return flights from mid-Germany] rumble in the air above us and we know that the attack on Berlin is over for that night. But we won't know the outcome 'til later. And there's the constant stabbing worry about the future . . .!"

Erich was able to come to Voerde for six days in December and help raise spirits. The little family celebrated a private Christmas Eve in their room before joining the others, with some singing and recorder playing, reading of the scriptures, a few presents (some recycled!), and stories.

In early March, 1944, Klara found a little time for another note in her daughter's album, while she was caring for Ulrich, who was in bed with the flu. She pasted in one of the red-rimmed, thin-paper postcards, which survivors of a heavy bombing attack could send to their families. This one reads, *as translated by me:*

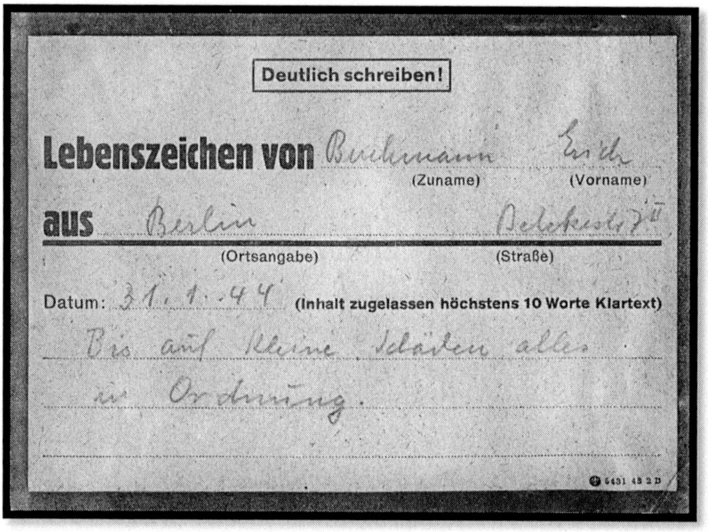
Deutlich schreiben!

Lebenszeichen von Buchmann Erich
(Zuname) (Vorname)

aus Berlin Betckestr. 7 II
(Ortsangabe) (Straße)

Datum: 31.1.44 (Inhalt zugelassen höchstens 10 Worte Klartext)

Bis auf kleine Schäden alles in Ordnung.

6431 43 2 D

Write legibly!
SIGN OF LIFE FROM: *Erich Buchmann.*
FROM: *Berlin, Betckestr. 7*
DATE: *January 1, 1944* (Use a maximum of 10 words, written clearly)
Except for minor damage everything is OK.

Klara also wrote: "Our daughter, at eleven, has little duties now, besides her long trek to school and back. For instance, she has to mend her own stockings. (*Who mends stockings anymore these days?*) She's good about keeping her clothes neat. On the whole, however, she's still a little girl and likes to play fantasy games with brother Ulrich and friends and cousins."

On March 9, Erich's younger brother, Werner, was killed in action on the Russian front. He had just turned thirty, having been drafted after his first year at the university, studying agriculture. He had married Ilse Weimann two years before, and the two had looked forward to starting a family when the war was over. His death was reported in a long letter by his superior, mourning his death, and stating that Werner had been killed by a direct hit from a bomb while addressing troops, who were retreating. Ilse never remarried. She continued her studies in medicine and became a doctor.

On April 1, 1944, Erich was promoted to *Ministerialrat* (a higher civil service position). He was now the head of his division of research for the navy. Klara and the children had to write and mail him their congratulations, since a visit was impossible.

I have found the original document of the promotion among my parents' papers. It is enclosed in a heavy, buff, paper folder, bearing in gold the eagle looking to his right with outspread wings. (Isn't it interesting that the eagle is a symbol both for Germany and the USA, as well as many other countries?) The raptor is perched on a wreath, which has the hooked cross, the swastika, in the middle. Inside is a second elegant document, signed by Hitler and Admiral Dönitz.

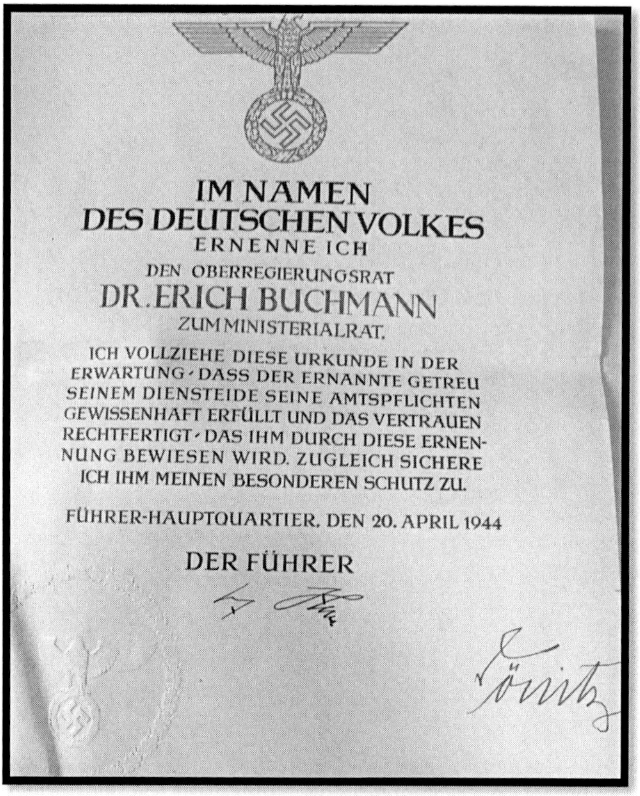

IM NAMEN
DES DEUTSCHEN VOLKES
ERNENNE ICH
DEN OBERREGIERUNGSRAT
DR. ERICH BUCHMANN
ZUM MINISTERIALRAT.

ICH VOLLZIEHE DIESE URKUNDE IN DER ERWARTUNG · DASS DER ERNANNTE GETREU SEINEM DIENSTEIDE SEINE AMTSPFLICHTEN GEWISSENHAFT ERFÜLLT UND DAS VERTRAUEN RECHTFERTIGT · DAS IHM DURCH DIESE ERNENNUNG BEWIESEN WIRD. ZUGLEICH SICHERE ICH IHM MEINEN BESONDEREN SCHUTZ ZU.

FÜHRER-HAUPTQUARTIER, DEN 20. APRIL 1944

DER FÜHRER

IN THE NAME OF
THE GERMAN PEOPLE

I AM PROMOTING
THE *OBERREGIERUNGSRAT*
DR. ERICH BUCHMANN

TO *MINISTERIALRAT.* [Head of a Section in Government]

I AM SIGNING THIS DOCUMENT IN THE EXPECTATION THAT THE ABOVE NAMED WILL FULFILL HIS DUTIES CONSCIENTIOUSLY, ACCORDING TO HIS OATH OF OFFICE, AND WILL JUSTIFY

THE TRUST PLACED IN HIM BY THIS RECOGNITION. AT THE SAME TIME, I ASSURE HIM OF MY SPECIAL PROTECTION.

Führer [Leader] Headquarters, April 20, 1944
THE FÜHRER

The document is signed in black ink by Adolf Hitler, in a downward-sloping, hard-to-read signature. On the bottom right, in a bold, easily read, blue ink signature (similar to the large one of John Hancock on the Declaration of Independence), is Dönitz, who was the admiral of the high command of the navy at the time.

From my own happy memories: there was a pony in Voerde, called Sonja, and sometimes we got to ride her. What fun! Papa was coming for Easter, finally. I missed him. My friend Helga was evacuated from Berlin to somewhere east. She wrote me a letter:

Dear Brigitte! Many thanks for your letter. I've gotten used to the school here and the teachers. My local girlfriend here, Ruth Dittrich, and I have a crush on our biology teacher, Fräulein Balzer. She sure makes biology more interesting than Herr Liefeldt ever did in Berlin. For English we have someone from the West. She pronounces words quite differently. For instance, for "go" she says "goh," while we learned "gouh." Do you remember Eva Voigt? She's here in my class with her crazy curls. Boy, does she show off! You wanted to know what we're doing in math right now? We're studying geometry.

Many greetings, Your Helga.

This is a scary memory: It was summer and Mutti called me into our room. She was lying on the bed, making little moaning sounds, and asked me to take the bedpan from under her and empty it. It was full of blood and clots!

Klara had had a miscarriage and required hospitalization for a while. The war raged on and enemy troops were now coming closer to the western side of the nearby Rhine. Klara wondered whether she and the children could safely stay so close to the border much longer, since they were not official residents of the area.

In Berlin and other German cities, the air attacks continued. My aunt Maria Buchmann, Kurt's wife, lived in Berlin during this time and she told me that the British Royal Air Force tended to do "saturation or carpet bombing" at night, using thousands of unguided bombs, aiming to destroy entire blocks of apartments, while the Americans did more "pinpoint bombing," striving for strategic targets during daylight over Hamburg, Essen, Frankfurt, Kiel, Bremen, Wesel, Leipzig, Augsburg, Stuttgart, Köln, and Berlin. I have researched and confirmed her story.

On June 6, 1944 ("D-Day"), American and British troops landed on French soil one hour before midnight. It was the largest amphibian force—150,000 men—in history. At the same time, Russian troops forged west toward Germany, which was now caught in the pincers of enemy troops on both sides.

On July 20, there was another of about two dozen assassination attempts on Hitler. A senior military officer, Colonel Claus Schenk von Stauffenberg, who had lost his left hand and fingers of his right hand in previous military engagements, left a bomb in a briefcase by Hitler's chair during a conference. Stauffenberg excused himself and left the room. Somehow, the briefcase was pushed under the heavy oak conference table. The bomb exploded. However, Hitler only suffered superficial wounds. He was elated about his survival and considered it the hand of fate for him to continue in his strategies. Stauffenberg and his collaborators were executed and the family members were imprisoned.

Millions of refugees from the East, fleeing from the Russians, poured into middle Germany, which was already largely destroyed. Hitler named Goebbels Reich director for total war mobilization. He and Albert Speer directed Germany's resources for the war and at the same time managed to keep most of the nation's utilities operating, food distributed, and housing arranged for the many who had lost their homes. According to one historian, Mark Weber, this was an achievement without historical parallel.

In the fall of 1944, Klara wrote, "Brigitte can't go to school anymore. It's too dangerous in railroad stations and on trains. Ulrich also is 'on vacation.' His teacher is sick and when he recovers he'll be drafted for home defense. I hope Papa can come briefly, as planned. We haven't seen him since Easter and we need to make a decision on whether to stay here or where else to go. I need to keep up my courage in this critical situation. Never have we needed a trust in God more than right now. May he help us."

I remember this: The last time I went to school, there was a very scary situation at the Voerde train station. We heard a plane come closer and lower, and then the pilot started to shoot at the train and us people. We dropped down and crawled under the railroad cars. One person was hurt. I went on to school, but after that day, Mutti wouldn't let me go anymore.

I hadn't even told her that another day, when I was walking home along the railroad tracks, I heard an enemy plane. It was a British engine; I could tell the difference. Then I heard the flak. I saw the plane catch fire and go spiraling down in black smoke. And then I saw the pilot floating down with his parachute. He landed in a tree! I ran away.

I also remember this: I was walking home from school on the street, when a plane came flying lower and lower. I jumped into the roadside ditch and made myself as flat as I could. I didn't get shot and the plane droned off. These strafing fighter planes would just show up at any time. After I got up again and was walking home, I had a strange experience. I noticed that somehow the danger and the knowledge that I could have died at any moment made everything around me more vivid. The grass was greener and more lush, the sky was bluer, the flowers and aromas were more intense, the trees more majestic, and the birdsong sweeter. Life was more precious and more appreciated when danger hovered close by.

When I got home, I changed my clothes and took off my shoes and ran around barefoot. My feet had become so tough that I could walk through a stubble field barefoot!

In November 1944, the Buchmann family made plans for Klara and the children to return to Berlin as soon as possible, since they were not officially local residents in Voerde. From Berlin, the plan was to find refuge in another area. Day after day in Voerde, the cannon thunder from the nearby front came closer and the air alarms became more frequent. The future looked very dark. How to get away, with luggage and two children, and very irregular and crowded trains?

Erich came and picked up his family. The travel by train from Voerde to Berlin was a nightmarish adventure. The usual five-hour trip lasted twenty-four hours, with frequent interruptions due to alarms, low-flying strafing planes, delays, and indescribable crowding.

Klara was so happy to be back in her own home, although she knew the stay would be temporary. Her novel *Unsere Tant' Marie* (*Our Auntie Marie*) was accepted for publication in *Dies Blatt gehört der Frau* (*This Magazine Belongs to the Woman*). Only one serial installment got printed and then the magazine stopped publication due to the war. The novel dealt with a single woman coping in life without job skills. Klara also sold the movie rights, but the war stopped that process also. (*Unfortunately, that novel has been lost.*)

I remember: In Berlin, I could go to school three days a week, but mostly we just took attendance, got started on something, and then the sirens went off and we had to go down into the air raid shelter. Sometimes we sang or played games, but mostly we just sat and hoped for the best. We really didn't have any classes to speak of. In the basement shelter, we could hear bombs if they were close by. They had a whining sound, starting at high pitch and descending lower and lower.

I found out later, from my physicist father, that a noisemaker was actually added to bombs by a special mechanism; the sound was not due to the bombs falling, but was intended as a fear-inducing factor.

When the steady howl of the "all-clear" siren sounded, we trudged back upstairs. It was very hard to get paper in those days, and what we got was very thin. Pens were rare and pencils didn't show up well on the poor-quality paper, and they often made the paper rip.

In the forest of Ardennes, on December 16, the German army penetrated the Allied lines in a surprise move, driving a "bulge" through them. The "Battle of the Bulge" was won by the superior Allied numbers. In the meantime, in the East, Russian troops continued to advance toward Germany and its capital, Berlin.

I remember: Mutti was homeschooling me now in geography, history, and English. I was practicing a Christmas carol on my recorder. The day before, we had gone to a Christmas party at Papa's work. It was a long trip on the streetcars, but it was worth it. Everything was decorated nicely; we got some presents and cookies and Stollen *(a German fruit cake), and then we sang carols. A lot of these new carols were quite beautiful, even though they didn't mention Jesus. (Under the Hitler regime, Christian carols were discouraged and sectarian new carols were published.)*

In the Berlin apartment, all four family members now had to sleep in one large bed in the master bedroom. Both of the children's bedrooms had been allotted to a refugee family from the East. Brigitte and Ulrich didn't mind; they liked the new people.

I remember: Mutti had asked me to get some bread. As during the entire winter, and also in the past, it was bitterly cold, gray, and windy. I was freezing again in my winter coat and my fingers were numb even though I was wearing mittens. Everything looked so depressing. There was hardly any food in the stores. Mutti got on her bicycle sometimes and bought or bartered with farmers for vegetables (especially potatoes) some bacon, eggs, and apples. We had lots of money, but nothing to buy with it. Mutti sometimes traded with cigarettes, too, but she was afraid to buy on the black market. I got to the store and used a coupon for bread. I was looking forward to my Bunter Teller *(colorful plate) at home in this time of Advent, with some nuts and Mutti's* Knusperchen *(an unbaked cookie made from oats, chocolate powder, almond flavoring, and a little sugar).*

Uncle Kurt came by to visit and brought an orange. He cut the peel like flower petals and gave each of us a section of the fruit. What a heavenly aroma and taste! What a treat! One orange for the whole family! And I remember it well because it was a rarity.

I remember thinking: That was our sixth wartime Christmas. Half of my life had been lived during that war.

CHAPTER 11

1945: Second evacuation from Berlin. Bad Frankenhausen. End of war. American troops enter. First Negroes seen. Fleeing from the Russians.

In early 1945, Berlin became a more and more dangerous place to be. Fourteen million refugees from the East, forced out by the Russians or leaving in fear of them, poured into the West, into already largely destroyed cities, including Berlin. Air raids continued day and night. Fortunately, Erich and some of his colleagues were finally able to arrange an evacuation of their families, although Erich himself had to stay in Berlin. The families were to go to a small spa town farther southwest, called *Bad Frankenhausen,* in Thüringen.

Klara wrote, "We're being evacuated from Berlin again and don't know whether we'll ever see our home again. Saying goodbye is so hard. Yet, compared to the suffering of the many, many refugees, we must be grateful. May God give us strength and protection."

A colleague of Erich's, Dr. Teutenberg, accompanied Klara, Brigitte and Ulrich. The train station was hellish. It was cold in early February, dark because of the blackout, and crowded. Klara was afraid that she and the children might get separated. She appreciated Dr. Teutenberg's forging ahead like an icebreaker and getting the family on the train early enough to secure seats for all of them. They had quite a bit of luggage with them since they did not know whether they would ever be able to return to their home. Klara saved the diaries and photo albums. *They have served as the main basis of this family memoir.*

Ulrich (Uli), age eight, wrote a little booklet about the trip, illustrated with watercolor pictures by his sister, Brigitte (Gitte), age twelve. Klara sent it to their papa, who preserved it.

I found it among the boxes of files. It is written in pencil on cheap, thin, yellowed paper, which Erich later had carefully pasted onto sturdier white paper. Uli wrote with the usual creative spelling of an eight-year-old, which I haven't attempted to translate.

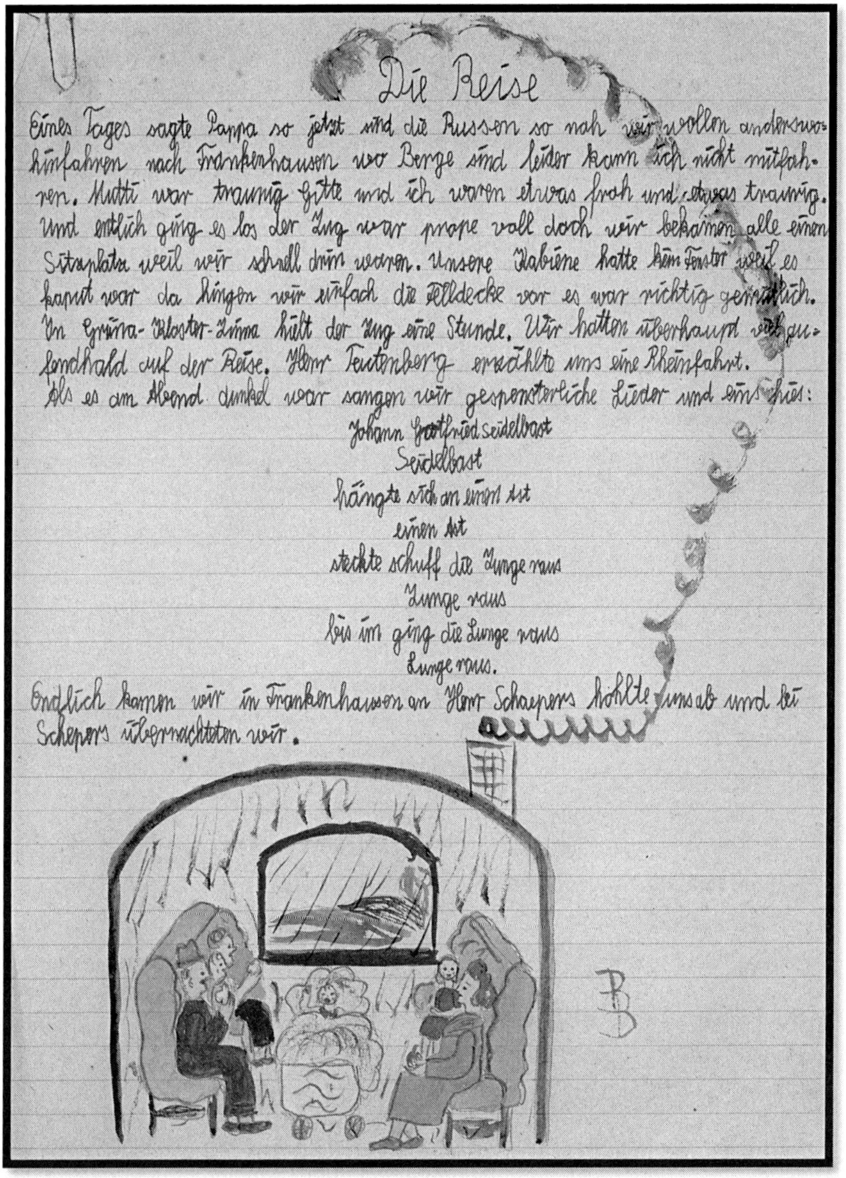

Die Reise

Eines Tages sagte Pappa so jetzt sind die Russen so nah wir wollen anderswo hinfahren nach Frankenhausen wo Berge sind leider kann ich nicht mitfahren. Mutti war traurig Gitte und ich waren etwas froh und etwas traurig. Und endlich ging es los der Zug war prope voll doch wir bekamen alle einen Sitzplatz weil wir schnell drin waren. Unsere Kabiene hatte kein Fenster weil es kaputt war da hingen wir einfach die Felldecke vor es war richtig gemütlich. In Grüna-Kloster-Linna hielt der Zug eine Stunde. Wir hatten überhaupt viel gusondhald auf der Reise. Herr Teutenberg erzählte uns eine Rheinfahrt. Als es am Abend dunkel war sangen wir gespensterliche Lieder und eins hieß:

Johann Gottfried Seidelbast
Seidelbast
hängte sich an einen Ast
einen Ast
steckte schnell die Zunge raus
Zunge raus
bis im ging die Lunge raus
Lunge raus.

Endlich kamen wir in Frankenhausen an Herr Schaepers hohlte uns ab und bei Schepers übernachteten wir.

THE TRIP, February 2, 1945

One day, Papa said, "Okay, now the Russians are so nearby that we have to go somewhere else, to Frankenhausen. You'll like it, because you'll see mountains.

Unfortunately, I can't come along." Mutti was sad. Gitte and I were a little happy and a little sad. And finally we got going to the *Anhalter Bahnhof* [Anhalt Train Station]. The train was stuffed full of people, but we all found a seat because we got inside early. Our compartment didn't have glass in the window and the wind was blowing. So Mutti and Dr. Teutenberg used our brown-and-white horsehide blanket to cover the window and it was really *gemütlich* [cozy] inside. Herr Teutenberg told us stories and later we sang spooky songs. There were a lot of long stops and delays, and Gitte and I slept a lot, but finally we saw light and looked out of the window, around the fur blanket, and saw that we were in Halle. We got out. My eyes boggled at the crowd, pushing and shoving. Dr. Teutenberg asked when a train would go to Sangerhausen. It was eight o'clock in the evening and at 8:30, there was supposed to be a train. But we heard an announcement that it was delayed by fifty minutes. Then the siren blew, alarm, and we went into the basement to the shelter. I fell asleep on Mutti's lap. Finally, I woke up because of the all-clear siren. We had been under alarm for three hours. The train had waited at the platform. We got on and found seats again and I fell asleep again. Dear Papa, we've gotten over the biggest part of the trip, but the worst is yet to come. Read on carefully.

I woke up in the morning. One station before Sangerhausen, the train stopped again for one hour and fifteen minutes. In the meantime, a *D-Zug* [rapid train] came into the station. We wanted to catch it, but it left too fast. We quickly hurried back into our slow train and waited. After another fifteen minutes, an *Arbeitszug* [work train] arrived; it was going to Sangerhausen. We asked whether we could go with them and the people said yes. And soon this train left. It was real slow and kept ringing a bell in every little station. Imagine, we were on a *Bimmelbahn* [local bell-ringing train]. Luckily we finally arrived in Sangerhausen. Dr. Teutenberg asked about a train to Brettleben. There was supposed to be one in six hours. We looked at the clock: 10:30 [a.m.] So we went into the waiting room. We had an alarm twice, but everything turned out all right. At four o'clock, the train arrived, and after a lot of running, we got into it. At 4:32, it left. We were all amazed that it was only two minutes late. After forty-five minutes, we arrived in Brettleben. Now we had another long, long wait for the next train, so we went for a walk in Brettleben. Finally, finally we made it to Bad Frankenhausen and we were met by Herr Schepers. We had been traveling for thirty-six hours. Ordinarily the trip would last about six hours. And now we saw some mountains!

We spent the night in the Schepers' house. Their kids and Gitte and I all slept in one room. It was very tight, of course, and before we could go to sleep, everyone needed to go to the toilet, but finally we all fell asleep. In the morning I heard Mutti calling us and I was confused 'til I remembered that we were not home. The Schepers kids were nice. In the second night, there was bad luck. I threw up all over the bed and Mutti and Frau Schepers had to clean everything up. The other kids watched and I was embarrassed.

After two days, we got a room in the *Kameradschaftshaus* [fellowship house]. The room was big and had a table, sofa, and chairs, plus beds. Behind the house, there was a locomotive and we played in it. We've had company often, sometimes Herr Gutmann, who brought us little treats to eat; sometimes Herr Teutenberg, who taught Gitte Latin; sometimes Frau Heimbrecht, the director,

> who also brought us some food. Every Sunday, we go to the movies. Mutti says, "We don't have *Kuchen* [cake], but we do have *Kinos* [movies] and they both start with a K." [These movies were mostly nature films; no American movies, of course.] One day a lot of visitors came from Berlin. Mutti cooked downstairs in the kitchen with all the other ladies and we had a great time. Someone played accordion and we sang many folk songs.

Klara had appended a little note of her own: "Dear Erich, just a short greeting. I have to run around a lot to get things settled. Anyhow, you've heard the essentials from Dr. Teutenberg on the phone. We're getting organized. I do hope we'll be able to return to Berlin before too long."

I feel sad when I read how much my mother was still hoping to return to her home. In retrospect, I become aware again that the war with its upheavals, difficult as it was for us children, was much harder on the adults. And I admire how my father and mother kept us children as protected as possible from the troubles.

Klara liked the beautiful, medieval spa town near the Kyffhäuser Mountains. A few days later, the family moved into old Fräulein Köhler's tiny, ancient house. They were given an apartment downstairs in the basement, with a bedroom for Uli and Gitte. Klara slept on the couch in the living room. Frl. Köhler came down often to visit with the refugees from the North and occasionally brought some food and ate and chatted with them. She spoke the local dialect, which the children sometimes had trouble understanding.

I remember: I was in another school again. I was getting mighty confused about history because we'd been studying different time periods in all my various schooling settings. I also noticed in math that memorizing my multiplication tables had not stuck with me, for lack of practice.

Those kids there again didn't want to become friends, especially with strangers from up north. Although the town was pretty, with its cobblestone streets and fountains and the grand cathedral and palace, it seemed cold and uninviting to me. When I walked to school I took one of three walking sticks with me for company. I'd cut them from some flexible willow tree branches. The biggest one I called Herr Reebock (Mr. Buck). The next biggest was Frau Ricke (Mrs. Doe), and the thinnest was Fräulein Zicke (Miss Fawn). I talked to my imaginary friends on my walks. I remembered Papa telling us a rhyme at bedtime: "Die kleinen Rehlein falten die Zehlein, halb acht. Gut' Nacht" *(The little deer fold their toes, seven thirty, goodnight). It was just too funny to think of deer folding their "toes."*

The alarms were getting bad there, too, and the front crept closer every day from the West. Almost every night, we had to get up and go to a bunker in the Gutshof Boerner, *a large farm, which was three minutes away. We just always went to bed dressed those days and had our suitcases ready at the door.*

How strange it is to be editing this chapter more than six decades later. How my life has changed and the world also! I'm proofreading this chapter while the World Cup of soccer (Fussball) *is playing on TV in the background, on Sunday, July 9, 2006. My three children, their spouses, and seven grandchildren are all watching in various places, along with billions of people worldwide, while the game is proceeding in the same stadium in Berlin, Germany, where the Olympics were held, with Hitler in attendance, in 1936. (Those were the same Olympics into which my father jokingly had said that he would enter me when I was two years old and climbing all over the furniture.) The final score at the World Cup, after ninety minutes of play plus two fifteen-minute overtimes: Italy 1, France 0 on a penalty kick. How fit those soccer players are, running all that time!*

I'm doing a final edit of this chapter in 2015. The delay is due to my happily full and busy life, which hasn't allowed time for reflecting on the past and writing about it. There have been many more wars. At this time, Syria is a bombed-out country with millions of refugees. A fundamentalist Islamist militant group called ISIS is killing other Muslims, Christians, Jews, and Westerners with the aim of establishing an Islamic State. There are wars in Africa and Ukraine. It never ends . . .

Back to 1945: There is no mention in Klara's or Erich's notes or letters, and I have no recollection of hearing about the horrible event that happened on February 13, 1945, when Allied bombers attacked Dresden, killing 135,000 civilians in one night! The terrible Dresden air raid was described by the American author Kurt Vonnegut Jr. in his book, Slaughterhouse-Five, *published in 1969. He was a prisoner of war who survived the fire in a bunker, which had once been a slaughterhouse. Dresden had been spared until then and had been considered a safe city because it had no military value, contained many internationally renowned art treasures, and held numerous refugees. The bombs and the ensuing firestorm destroyed most of the city. The most gruesome scene of the book in my memory is that of schoolgirls who tried to save themselves from the flames by climbing into a water tower and were boiled to death.*

On March 10, American flyers firebombed Tokyo. Many of the wooden houses ignited like tinder, and eighty to a hundred thousand people died, mostly civilians.

Klara and Erich saved some letters from these turbulent times when they were separated. I found carbon copies, which they always made, in those boxes in my basement. Erich wrote to Klara on March 16, 1945 (less than two months before the end of the war in Europe):

> I'm writing this letter from Kiel, where I'm visiting the CPVA (Chemistry and Physics Research Department). Much has happened; more in the Rhineland now than toward the East. I think often of our family in Voerde. How are they doing? We have no news of them and can only hope that all is well. In Düsseldorf, where we met sixteen years ago, it seems to be quiet at the moment.

I'm overwhelmed by sadness to think of the tragedy that befell Klara and Erich in their young family life. Their world was put in ruin.

Erich continued:

> However, a lot of bombing is happening in Wesel, where Brigitte went to school last year. I've packed a suitcase of things for you. Uli's shoes weren't ready. Gutmann and Seybart will take the bag to you. I'm trying hard to finagle a trip to see you. Schede is no longer here since he's

been commandeered to a different work location, and that makes it hard for me to leave. Next time I'm in Berlin I'll pack another suitcase with the things you've listed.

I'm glad you're somewhere where I can get news fairly often and find out how you're all doing. Soon it'll be spring and you'll see how beautiful the region there will be at that time. Gitte and Uli seem to be adjusting; and you, too, according to Teutenberg, seem to have become accustomed to your new surroundings, better than I had judged from your earlier letters. I can't report anything else from Kiel or Berlin.

Many, many warmest greetings to you all,
Papa

I remember: We were really looking forward to Easter, because Mutti had said that we'd get some nice things. Finally, finally it was Sunday, the first of

April. We woke up very early, but weren't allowed to get up until eight o'clock. And then we got to see our Easter presents. I got a concertina (a small accordion), a pencil, and a block of paper. For Uli, I had written and illustrated a little storybook, Widdely, das Engelkind *(*Widdely, the Naughty Little Angel*). (This booklet has recently been published in English and is available on amazon.com.) I also made him a* Kasperletheater *(a puppet theater made from a cardboard box with cutout figures of* Kasperle *[a clownish character], a witch, and other characters). And Mutti gave Uli some writing paper and some story booklets. At ten o'clock, we went on an Easter egg hunt in Frau Heimbrecht's garden. In the afternoon, we saw a movie,* Wiesenzwerge (Meadow Dwarfs). *And in the evening, we had lots of visitors and someone brought us some cherry preserves! A wonderful Easter! In a few days, Papa was supposed to come and visit. We were so happy, but we knew he could only stay a day.*

During March 1945, the American army crossed the Rhine River in several places, while the Russians kept advancing from the East. Magdalene's (Erich's younger sister's) husband, Karl Fey, was reported missing in action. (*Magdalene never remarried. She was a teacher and lived with her sister, Ruth; her husband, Heinrich; and their children, Uwe and Swantje. She died at age sixty-two of stomach cancer and willed her estate to Ruth.*)

Another letter from Erich to Klara, on April 4, reads:

> I have the firm intention to come visit again and perhaps I'll succeed. Enclosed are two writing notebooks for the kids and an advance of eight hundred Mark. Who knows how everything will develop now. Things are happening at a tempo I'd never imagined possible. If I cannot get all the way to you, then we'll certainly be separated for quite some time. I hope to God that it will not be for too long. It's a comfort to me that you look to the future in a poised and confident manner.
>
> All our letters now are tinged with a mood of sadness and goodbye. Who knows what will happen; but I strongly hope to find you and the children again, and in good health. Otherwise, we will hold on to that which is our only comfort in life and in death. It is my strong desire to impart to the children a sense of this attitude toward eternity, and to entrust all of you to the mercy of our Lord.
>
> Of what use are words at this time! We have lived together for many years and know each other well, and also our desires. I am happy that our children are with a mother like you. May God hold his hand over all of you!

On April 7, 1945, apparently after a short visit to Frankenhausen, Erich wrote to Klara:

> We've arrived safely here in Gusten; everything went according to plan. To bicycle from Frankenhausen to

Sangerhausen was quite some effort; my leg muscles are just beginning to recover. I wanted to call you, but the post office [where the public phones were located] couldn't get through because of electricity rationing. Too bad. I'm glad to have made the considerable effort to come to Bad Frankenhausen. Although goodbyes are always difficult, it was a good thing to see all of you once more and know that you are well and how you're situated. We didn't finish deciding about possible meeting places if there's too much turmoil and Berlin is not a possibility. If the Russians come to Berlin, then by all means stay as long as possible in Frankenhausen. I myself will always try to make contact there. Contact in Berlin will perhaps also be possible. If not, the other meeting points to consider are Voerde, Düsseldorf, and Werne, your hometown. Somehow, I have the hopeful feeling that we will get together again.

At present, we can't escape the whole mess. And somehow everything happens en masse: train travel, meals, duty, saying goodbyes. The group is trump; the individual is nothing. Everything is in a whirlwind. How will it look a year from now, when separated families are still searching for each other and when missing persons may be considered lost or dead? How much we yearn for a life of peace and order, as we had envisioned it years ago. Now, everything the mass does is a force one must follow if one does not wish to perish. It's a result of industrialization and the technological way of our life and time. We're not individuals anymore; we sit in a home where the next person lives a bare ten paces away. Whoever breaks out of the mass pronounces his own sentence, since the group cannot tolerate such an action.

In my own veins there flows too much farmer's blood. I carry genetic material from a time when our ancestors lived on their own land, which they could stride freely, and where they felt they were their own masters. That's why, especially now, I constantly feel the undercurrents of my longing for house and hearth, for forest and meadow. These feelings are emphasized by the coming of spring. The tension of contrasts will certainly generate new wells of creativity.

At this time, we have, on the one hand, the last desperate fighting of a hard-hit people for their existence, and on the other hand, the calm, orderly process of nature, which lets spring appear in all its glory without diminution of this wonder of creation. The flowers will come up and bloom without regard for us and whether we may have perished or survived.

Just as strongly we feel the powerful word of the Bible, that all of humanity and nature is longing for salvation. Everything is not as it should be; a curse lies on everything. The good we wish to do we don't do; how does that apply to the happenings in the world in the last years? All we wanted was happiness and peace, and we had imagined it so clearly. Instead of that, we are separated, we have lost close family members in the war, and we have had a life of strife and unrest.

All this forces us to eliminate our bourgeois longings and to recheck our opinions about many things. After all, what has happened that touches us so powerfully? Wars have always been and always will be; nations have come and gone. In short, life arises and disappears. And all that in a framework where next to the beautiful there is always the ugly, next to the good the bad, next to love, hate. How hard God is testing us! We have to experience these contrasts to a degree that is not often asked of humans. And how does this test affect us? It is difficult to say right now. I feel that many have a leaning toward belief in miracles, but not yet toward a faith in God.

> Boundless fear and worry is moving through the land and is justified by the events which have befallen us in the East. But all that is not yet resulting in faith, in a bending to the judgment and sovereignty of God. And it is difficult, since we have many good works to our credit. For myself it is all very hard, but on the other hand I'm not surprised. According to the results, we will not fall into the error of thinking that we can force God into giving us a fate that would please us; we will not repeat the error of the theologians. God wishes to be with us in only mercy and faith.

I have translated my father's letter as well as I can, but nevertheless I cannot say that I fully understand it. He is speaking from a Weltanschauung *(world view) of philosophy and religion, which I find hard to align myself with today. Under the disastrous circumstances of destruction at the end of a lost war, I am particularly amazed by his faith in a loving and merciful God.*

I once asked my father whether we were related to Frank Buchman, the American Lutheran minister from Pennsylvania who founded the Oxford Group in England in the 1920s. He answered, "I think so, distantly." Frank Buchman was quite renowned. He renamed his movement "Moral Re-Armament" in 1938 and was valued in many countries, including by Franklin D. Roosevelt in the United States. However, Reinhold Niebuhr and Dietrich Bonhoeffer thought that he was naïve in believing he could influence world leaders, including Hitler. After World War II, however, he helped facilitate reconciliation between France and Germany and many other countries.

On the next day, April 8, 1945, Erich wrote to his almost thirteen-year-old daughter.

> Dear Brigitte,
>
> Now your Papa is back in Berlin, after having seen you all briefly for a few hours in Frankenhausen. I was glad that all of you, but especially you, are healthy and happy. I myself arrived in Berlin a little tired, but otherwise fine. I can't tell when I can come to see you

again; it could be soon, but it could also take a long time. Therefore, I'm going to try to get this letter to you.

I've always been glad to see that you have an open mind for everything. Keep that up—it's a good trait for all of your life. You just have to watch that at the same time you remain modest and show respect for older people. And above all, we mustn't forget to be thankful for all we have been given, be that food, drink, talent, etc.

Keep in your memory all beautiful and meditative hours, and don't let any unpleasant experiences spoil your character. Your parents have given you so much and wish to continue to do so. Never think small; always think of the big picture. Don't get caught up in trash or gossip. Instead, read a good book; that's a better way to spend time.

And remember above all that the meaning of life cannot be explained on a material basis; it has a metaphysical background. Don't let that connection be broken by outward appearances or matters. You cannot make judgments based on those by others; you will have to form your own. Parents cannot save their children; children must build their own lives. We, as parents, want to provide good conditions and advice. The commandments of God must be the guiding lines for life, following our merciful God's direction and worshipping him.

Well, Brigitte, Mutti will be able to tell you better about all this.

Be well mannered and good and always nice to Mutti and Uli,

Your Papa

Erich wrote a separate letter on the same day to his almost nine-year-old son.

Dear Uli, now that you're the only man with Mutti and Brigitte, you have the important job to take care of them, since I can't be there all the time. You're always nice and helpful to Mutti. Keep that up. What more do I need to tell a capable young man like you?

Too bad that we had so little time together. Next time when I come, we'll go exploring and look around the area, visit some caves, and make sure that all robbers have been chased away. And maybe there are other things to do over there.

Well, I've written a lot to each of you. When will I hear from you again? Please keep writing.

Warm hugs and kisses,
Your Papa

PS. Tell Mutti I'm sending a package with two pairs of tennis shoes, a flashlight, and a tablecloth.

Uli wrote a letter to his Papa on the twelfth of April:

The last few days there've been lots and lots of air raid alarms. We had to be in the basement at Fräulein Köhler's almost all the time. Often, we also just lay under the table when we heard the bombs making that whining noise as they came down. To go outside and play is out of the question.

Yesterday, on the eleventh of April, it was really bad. We went to the bunker at Boerner's farm. Finally, after six hours, Mutti and I went out to try and get some food from home. But a woman met us on the street and said, "It's the enemy alarm!" The siren just kept going and going. So I ran back, but Mutti went to our rooms to get more of our luggage and some food and then we all slept in the bunker. We had one little stump of candle left. There were a lot of people in the bunker. Lots of crying kids and snoring persons. We slept for a while on the sacks of potatoes. Then we heard shots and the rolling of heavy tanks from 4:00 to 6:00 p.m. When it got quiet, we looked out carefully and saw some people moving around. Frankenhausen didn't have any defense, so it was all over.

The Americans were here, and there were a lot of Negroes! We've never seen any before. We became friends quickly. Gitte could talk to them a little because she's learned some English. They gave us Hershey bars and chewing gum and some real coffee for Mutti. They also had three dogs: Brownie, Queen, and Snowball. One guy sat in the guardhouse, and every evening he cooked himself a good dinner over a little fire. We could see that fire every evening and night.

My own memory: These Americans played with a funny-looking ball. It was brown and elliptical. They called that a football, although they didn't kick it with their feet. The Negroes looked just like the Moors I remember seeing in the store windows, advertising some kind of chocolate. I never actually saw that chocolate, of course, because in the war there wasn't any available. The Negro soldiers here spoke English, but I had a hard time understanding them. They did seem very friendly, though.

Klara wrote only a very brief note into the children's photo albums:

Finally, finally . . . Enemy alarm for five minutes, then entry of the Americans! Quieter times now. I work at the large farm, in exchange for eggs and some other produce. We eat a lot of cracked eggs. There are *Schwarze* (blacks) across the street. These days I often have a *Kaffeeklatsch* (coffee hour), with real coffee now, at noon with Fräulein Köhler. We're having an infestation of mice in our rooms. Springtime here is lovely; the lilacs are heavy with blooms and scent everywhere. The garden gazebo has fragrant jasmine vines twining all around it.

I remember: Fräulein Köhler had a lot of old magazines that she let me read. These dated from the 1920s and '30s. I loved to look at the fashions. Imagine—at that time they thought it was very unfeminine to show any bones. For instance, you shouldn't see the collarbones. Also, you shouldn't show any space between your thighs from the crotch to the knees. Skinny me wouldn't have fit into those times at all.

I liked sitting in the gazebo, inhaling the strong scent of jasmine, enjoying the mottled sun and shade, and playing with a visiting cat. The air raids were over, thank God!

Mutti brought home a lot of eggs. I noticed that she had developed little yellowish spots the size of rice grains under her eyes. (These were probably cholesterol deposits.)

On April 9, just two weeks before the Allies liberated the concentration camp, Dietrich Bonhoeffer, the dissident Protestant pastor, was executed on Hitler's order. Many of his family members were also killed. Bonhoeffer had had the opportunity, before the war, to stay in the United States at Union Theological Seminary in New York, where he studied and worked under Reinhold Niebuhr. However, he had decided he needed to be in his country and help it through difficult times and he returned to Germany. An outspoken pacifist in imitation of Jesus, he had made the difficult and dangerous decision in the last phase of the war that it was morally more correct to kill a dictator than to continue working ineffectually to help Jews and others who were persecuted by Hitler.

I have often wondered whether I have Bonhoeffer's kind of courage. He did not have children yet. For me, since I'm a mother, it is clear that I would probably not endanger my family and children with a politically and personally suicidal action.

Another person who decided to return to Germany from England and the USA just prior to the war was the physicist Werner Heisenberg, discoverer of the uncertainty principle. He, too, had been invited to stay in the United States, but felt that he would have to be in his homeland during the conflict in order to help his country rebuild after the war.

An excellent and thought-provoking play, Copenhagen *by Michael Frayn, written in 1998, deals with Heisenberg and his mentor, the Danish physicist Niels Bohr, and describes the moral choices people had to make during these difficult times. In the play, Heisenberg visits Bohr in German-occupied Copenhagen and attempts to engage him to warn nations about the potential dangers of building bombs utilizing nuclear fission. He himself is working on the nuclear reactor project in Germany, but is certain that the necessary resources will not be available there to develop a bomb.*

Bohr and his wife show disdain for Heisenberg's continued work in Nazi Germany. However, Heisenberg feels that he has to return to his country and see it through the difficult time. He is not a member of the Nazi party, and he also helps Bohr and his family and hundreds of Jews to escape via boat from German-occupied Denmark to neutral Sweden. On the other hand, Bohr leaves for America and joins the Manhattan Project in Los Alamos late in 1943, helping to develop the atomic bombs, which were used over Japan in 1945 and killed hundreds of thousands of civilians.

On April 11, American troops liberated the Buchenwald concentration camp. The photos of emaciated prisoners, Jews, communists, and others enraged the world after initial disbelief and shock. *I don't recollect hearing anything about this.*

On the twelfth, FDR (Franklin Delano Roosevelt) died, and Harry S. Truman became president in the United States.

On the thirtieth, Adolf Hitler died by his own order of a gunshot in his Berlin bunker, along with Eva Braun, whom he had married just recently. *A gripping movie,* Der Untergang (Downfall) *depicts the last ten days of Hitler.* The Soviets advanced and occupied Berlin. Later, Berlin was divided into four occupation zones, although the city lay in Soviet-controlled territory. Germany itself was also divided into four occupation zones: American, French, British, and Soviet.

On May 1, Goebbels and his wife Magda killed their six children and themselves by poison. According to Hitler's will, the new *Führer* became Admiral Karl Doenitz, a former submarine commander, who had succeeded Erich Räder. Doenitz "served" for one week and ratified the unconditional surrender of Germany on May 7, now remembered as VE Day. This denoted the end of World War II in Europe, after five years, eight months, and at least sixty million dead.

I remember my papa mentioning the names Räder and Doenitz. By then, my father's civil-service rank was equivalent to that of vice admiral in the navy, so he may have had contact with them, especially during those turbulent last weeks in Berlin. I wish, I wish I'd become interested in family history earlier so that I could have asked many more questions.

PART THREE

How Our Family Lived in Germany During the Post-War Years

1945–1948

Germany Post-WWII

Baltic Sea
North Sea
Dänisch-Nienhof
Kiel
Schleswig-Holstein
Bremerhaven
British Zone
Lüneburger Heide
Berlin
Hameln
Wesel
Voerde
North Rhine-Westphalia
Soviet Zone
Düsseldorf
Bad Frankenhausen
Thuringia
Dresden
Hesse
Frankfurt
Rhineland-Palatinate
French Zone
American Zone
Bavaria
Landshut
Munich

CHAPTER 12

1945: Fleeing from Frankenhausen and the Russians. 1946: Life in the British camp for German scientists and their families, in Dänisch-Nienhof.

Klara wrote to Erich on May 27, 1945.

Dear Erich and Papa,

Perhaps there will be an opportunity tomorrow to get this greeting to you with someone. All three of us are well. It's quiet here now and everything is functioning fairly normally. Some food supplies are coming in. We feel relatively comfortable here, considering the circumstances. All of us women help each other. In the afternoons, I work at the big farm Boerner, helping with sales; that gives me extra eggs and vegetables. During that time, the children play in the garden. I wonder how you are doing? We think of you often and pray every evening for our Papa. May God protect you.

Among my parents' papers, I found the following letter from Erich to Klara. It was dated June 12, 1945, and written in an urgent, almost desperate manner. Erich was now in Dänisch-Nienhof, a beach resort area near Kiel, in the British-occupied portion of Germany. A camp had been established here for certain German scientists, under British command.

Dear Klara and Dear Children,

I hope this letter will safely get into your hands and find you well. I'm trying to use any opportunity I find to get news about myself to you, but I don't know whether any of my letters have gotten through to you.

I haven't heard from you since early April, two and a half months ago, and just hope that you've survived everything until now and have enough to eat.

At this time, I have only one urgent wish: namely, that you try as soon as possible to get out of Frankenhausen. Since I don't know the conditions there, I can't give you any specific advice, but I believe that it is of the utmost importance that you escape, never mind how. In the end, it is unimportant whether you can take much or little with you. Since I'm in the British occupation zone, it's very important to me to know that you should also be in it.

I think it might be best if you try to take the children and go to Voerde. I know that you will get food there; everything else must be put on the back burner at this time. Just use any opportunity you can find to get out of the Thüringen zone for now. Perhaps you can take some belongings to a town nearby where they could be stored temporarily. Here in Schleswig-Holstein (*the province in which Kiel and Dänisch-Nienhof are located*), it is also unclear what will happen, but if you can find any possibility of getting here, that's preferable to staying where you are.

Don't take my words lightly. I know why I'm urgently begging you. Basically, I'm assuming that this letter will not find you there anymore because you've already left. On the other hand, judging by our previous talks in Berlin, there is a possibility that you're still hesitating. We can't predict the future, but I sincerely hope that my proposals find you receptive.

I am, as before, in a camp under English occupation, with other scientists. I can't complain. We have good accommodations and plenty to eat. I've even gained some weight. I continue to work as director of the CPVA (*Chemistry and Physics Research Station*), and my old colleagues are also here so that we can talk about many things. We report to the Royal Navy. Immo is here and asks, if possible, that you contact his wife and urge her to leave the area. According to the map, I propose the following route: Frankenhausen—Sondershausen or Nordhausen—Göttingen—Northeim—Driburg—Paderborn—Hamm, and so on. You're familiar with the area. Even if you escape in a northerly direction, it's best to go to Göttingen first. Since Dr. Rahlfs is writing his wife also to go there, perhaps you can discuss all this with her and find transportation together. Fritz Schepers is also deciding on a similar proceeding. You can convey my greetings to him and urge him to follow the same advice.

I don't know whether there are any men left there to help you. But in all your considerations, please remember that you have little time left and it's much more important to me that you save your lives than any material things. I believe that you understand me completely. Well, this is all for the part I wanted to tell you above all else.

You can imagine how much I'd like to be there with you, especially right now. I'd much rather be living with you, walk with the kids, and stretch my legs under your table. But all that just can't be at this time. We will all have to get used to the fact that we must put many personal wishes aside.

Because of your talent to cope with all situations of life, I have full confidence in the future for you and our children. We can't think too much of "what-ifs." I believe we can't manage that at the moment. We have to try to get firm ground under our feet again as soon as possible. Your knowledge of English, which is in great demand now, should be very helpful.

For myself, I can only say that I'm totally tied up here and can't predict what will happen from day to day. But I'll feel a lot better if I know that you are out of Thüringen. I remember many a conversation we've had and things others have said. But everything is much, much worse than I ever considered possible. I often think how good it is that we have a *Weltanschauung* (view or philosophy of life) that is not dependent on external things and that accepts that all happenings come from the hand of God.

Since I don't know whether you received my earlier letter, I'll tell you briefly what I know about my brothers. Ewald is in Pelzerhaken with his wife and children. Ernst came along to Thüringen; I don't know where; his family is in Bad Eilsen. Kurt is in Berlin; I have no further news. And where are all our many other family members and friends; what is their fate? We are all suffering so much pain. Who would have thought this possible in the past?

Dear Klara, stay well and try to see what can be done. This mail is going by a special messenger; I hope that it works out. I had to write this suddenly and am pressed for time, that's why I'm writing rather haphazardly. Give the kids greetings from their Papa, who would rather take them into his arms and give them a kiss than write letters such as this. I'm often with you in my thoughts and hope that it will be granted to us to see each other again. Please give my regards to all our friends there. Kids: I'm sending you a kiss, for Brigitte one on her nose and for Ulrich one on his ear. I'm sure you're both behaving yourselves and helping Mutti as much as you can.

Your Erich and Papa

It is clear, in retrospect, that although he couldn't mention it directly, Erich had heard from the British camp commander that the Americans were going to withdraw from the Frankenhausen area and let the

Russians move in and take over. It is also clear that he had heard of dreadful things happening to civilians, especially women, under Russian occupation and was very afraid for Klara and the children.

I remember it well: It was mid-June of 1945, and we were leaving Bad Frankenhausen very early in the morning in a large, open truck with no cover on it. We were six or seven families all together in two trucks, all of us originally from Kiel, with all the goods we had left. Mutti counted eighteen pieces of luggage for us: clothes, household items, and papers. I was glad that we were leaving and looked forward to seeing Papa again. I was sitting in the back of the truck, facing forward, with the wind in my face and blowing my hair. My hair was still very blond. When I was a baby, it was so fair that Mutti was embarrassed because it looked as if I had very little hair. So she always put a little hat on me. Because I'd heard that story so often, I was never really able to be happy with my blond hair. I guessed Mutti would have preferred a little girl with darker eyes and hair. However, at this moment, the wind in my hair and face gave me a feeling of looking forward to the future unafraid.

We drove and drove. The countryside was rural and pretty, but all the towns lay in horrible rubble. It was sad and depressing. Seeing all this destruction of my country was crushing my happiness. In the evening, we stopped at a farm. After some negotiations, the farmer allowed us to sleep in his barn on the straw. We were all exhausted and used the outhouse quickly, then immediately lay down. My eyes were smarting. The next morning Mutti looked at me and said, "Oh, my goodness, your eyes are so red!" I'd gotten conjunctivitis from the wind drying me out. Now I went and sat at the front of the open truck bed with my back against the cab.

We drove through the pretty heather in the Lüneburger Heide, heading north toward Kiel, where I was born. When we finally got there, we had a big shock—all was destroyed and in ruins! Our old home was gone, too! It was so hard to see this that we were glad when the truck drove on farther north to Dänisch-Nienhof. This was where our fathers and husbands were interned in a camp for scientists run by the British occupation forces. (Germany was divided into four occupation sectors: American, British, French, and Russian.) It was too dark to see much this evening; Papa and the other men met us at the truck and we hugged and kissed. Then the men unloaded. We entered a long, one-story wooden building, where our family had been allocated two rooms. No time or energy to unpack; we just ate a little something and fell down on the beds and slept.

Klara wrote in Brigitte's album:

> July 1945. Yet another place to live! The last weeks in Frankenhausen were full of worry about Papa and the future. Then I received Papa's letter, delivered to me by hand on June 16. The very next morning, at 6:00 a.m., we had an opportunity to leave via a large, open truck, along with several other families. The drive was actually through some very pretty landscapes. However, after seeing the bombed-out towns and then our former hometown Kiel, and the unbelievable destruction there, it was good to drive on north into a more rural environment.
>
> Here in Dänisch-Nienhof, our Papa is working in his old workplace with his colleagues, under British occupation, and seems happy. We are interned with him and quite content. We're in the women's and families' quarters in two rooms and Papa also has an office elsewhere. Inside this camp we have full freedom, although there's a sentry at the gate, but we can also travel to Kiel and other places with prior permission. This is a beautiful spot, three hundred acres large, a former resort. According to the name, the area must have been Danish at one time. The *Schloss* (chateau), where Papa's office is located, is lovely, except that someone painted it camouflage green toward the end of the war. There's a little lake in front of it. It's only a few minutes on a trail through the woods to the *Steilküste* (steep coast/cliff) and beach and ocean (the Baltic Sea).
>
> The children are happy here in their green, safe surroundings. Both are having swimming lessons, given by some of the British officers, but not much other

schooling yet. Brigitte has some math and also art lessons in watercolors with Professor Wigge.

The war is over in Europe, and we lost. We have to try to marshal all our reserves of strength to make a new beginning. Our home and goods in Berlin? Our money in the bank? We will probably never see any of it again. But if we can live together as a family, if Papa can work somehow and somewhere, then we'll be grateful. The time of terror and horror and the continuous destruction of the war is over. Now we must build a new peaceful future. God will help us with this and we have to muster our own courage.

We have all become poor and homeless. May the future bring our children a new home in peace.

As I translate this typewritten note pasted into my photo album by my mother, I am blown away by the spunk, the courage, and the lack of self-pity and complaining of my parents. After years of war, air raid terror, and evacuations, they showed their children an attitude of hope and determination. I only wish that I might have become interested in family history earlier, read all the notes, asked questions, and expressed to Mutti and Papa my admiration and deep gratitude.

I remember: My scalp itched and I had a cribbly feeling. Uli also had this problem. We were examined and—ugh—guess what? We all had head lice, as did the other families that came with us. Must have picked them up when we slept so close together on the straw in that farmer's barn. Now we had to use a special shampoo, but that alone didn't do the trick. Every day, we had to sit at the table, with a sheet of white paper in front of us, and lean forward to comb our hair with a fine-tooth comb. That got the little nits out. It was awful. I sat in a movie one day—the British officers show one every week, usually American—and I could just feel the little monsters crawling through my hair. I also had some boils on my knees that didn't heal well. Pus kept coming out. (Antibiotics were not available at that time.)

Otherwise we were fine. I didn't like our large, wooden house—the former foresters' cottage—because it was painted deep brown, looked like a barracks, and sat in the woods, so it was always shaded and rather dark. But the area outside—oh, I loved it there! The woods were mostly beech trees, Buchen. *I wondered whether our name, Buchmann, was related to beeches. Could have also derived from* Buch *(book), or* Busch *(bush). The beeches' elegant, smooth, and silvery trunks reached tall into the sky, with the serrated, pretty leaves forming a light-green canopy that filtered the sun. There would be lots of beechnuts in the fall. There were some cute red squirrels there and quite a few birds. No deer, no foxes, no rabbits—they'd all been hunted or trapped and eaten during the famine of the war and of the present. Going through the woods—which was easy, since there was little undergrowth—I came to the* Steilküste *(steep cliff). It was light in color. I thought it was because the woods were actually on a large dune. I ran down the wooden stairs to the beach and then there was the ocean—endless, beautiful, often blue, always changing! Going back, I scrambled up the bluff like a mountain goat.*

Now I was getting some private lessons with Professor Wigge, one of the scientists in Papa's group. He was teaching me geometry in such a fun way that it became my favorite subject. He had me cutting out triangles and squares so that I could prove to myself that "a^2 plus b^2 equals c^2." Mutti was doing some German and English with me. I also went on outings with Dr. Wigge, and we painted the Schloss, the woods, the cliff, and the ocean, using watercolors. That was great fun, too. Prof. Wigge was doing an oil painting of me. I was looking straight out, with blue eyes and blond braids, in a white blouse and red jumper, with trees and ocean behind me. (I still have that painting and it hangs in my bedroom hall.)

And there was a woman there in the camp who was a sculptor. She was doing a bust of me in clay that had a white finish, with my braids up on my head. She said my profile was like that of Nefertiti, the Egyptian pharaoh's wife, whose name means "the Beautiful One." (A famous, strikingly painted bust of Nefertiti is in a museum in Berlin. I still have my white bust, also. It sits on a cabinet in my living room.)

Several times, Mutti sent me to a farmer in the neighborhood for milk. It was quite a long walk and my shoes were worn. It jarred my whole body to walk on the street without any cushioning. At the farmer's house,

I knocked on the front door. The woman of the house came out and took me to the barn. Then she'd milk one of the cows and let the warm milk flow into the metal jug I'd brought along. Occasionally, she'd let me try milking. It wasn't as easy as I thought. You had to strip the tit just right, from the area closest to the udder down to the tip, before the milk would come out. You also had to watch that the cow didn't get irritated and kick. That warm, fresh milk really did taste good!

Occasionally, I was asked to watch a little baby girl. I had to walk through the woods and then across a wide meadow. On the right was the endless expanse of ocean and on the left were flat fields as far as I could see. I felt free when I was out on that meadow. There were some concrete bunkers and other defensive military structures, both on the meadow and down on the beach. They were quite broken up—too old to date from the recent war. I don't recall who lived in the little brick house where the wind always blew. The baby girl was quite sweet. I played with the baby endlessly and really enjoyed taking care of her.

Two world-changing events happened in August 1945. *There was no comment on this in my parents' papers, just as the bombings of Dresden and Hamburg had not been mentioned, nor the Holocaust findings of the concentration camps. At first, I was surprised at these omissions, but now I realize that in my daily calendars, over the years, I also seem to neglect noting down elections, hurricanes, and other important events, even wars, and just list daily family schedulings.*

On August 6, the United States dropped the first atomic bomb on Hiroshima, Japan, and on August 9, the second one on Nagasaki. Between one hundred fifty thousand and one hundred ninety thousand people were killed, half of them on the first day from burns and crushing injuries and the others later from radiation effects. No other atomic bomb has ever been used again. Japan surrendered within weeks and signed the official unconditional surrender on September 2.

World War II was over—the deadliest war ever. Ironically, just twenty-seven years earlier, World War I had been dubbed "the war to end all wars."

The numbers reported of military and civilian casualties in this catastrophic conflict vary wildly, depending not only on different source materials, but also depending on when the statistics were evaluated. For instance, Chinese losses were not immediately available, but very large, at least 20 million.

It was estimated that total deaths ranged between 60 and 80 million people, including 11 million concentration camp victims from Nazi-run camps, 6 million of them Jewish. Deaths in Soviet-run gulags were also very numerous, as were deaths of displaced persons and persons killed by bombs. All statistics indicated that civilian losses were larger than military losses!

Klara wrote in her daughter's album on October 17, "The woods in the park are showing color and the leaves rustle on the ground when we walk through this magic forest. The view of the sea is always changing. And we're still here, in the foresters' cottage, along with the Rahlfs and the Neumanns. Each family has two rooms. We're making do and are grateful to be able to live here this coming winter."

I remember: I was sitting with Uli in the golden evening sun on the steps of the red brick building where the Brits were going to show a movie soon. The evening made me feel melancholy. Where were we heading as a family? Where was my life going? What was the purpose of it, anyhow? I was thirteen now and didn't have any idea of what the future would bring. The day was coming to an end and so what?

But soon the movie started and it distracted me. I loved Richard Burton. He looked so virile, and yet self-controlled, but his expression was one of pain, as if it hurt him to hold back his full, loving ardor.

On December 25, 1945, Klara wrote into Brigitte's album:

> It's five o'clock in the evening, our first Christmas Day in peacetime since 1938. How much horror, sadness, and terror has happened in the world since I last wrote at Christmas in a time of peace, seven years ago!

> With great thanks to God, we're experiencing this year's salvation celebration. The calm winter here gives us new energy, which we urgently need after the fearful years just past. We still have plenty of worries: Where will we be going in the spring? How are we to exist? But today these questions and fears shall be silent.
>
> We cut the Christmas tree ourselves in the woods. Our room looks festive, with five candles on the tree and a nativity scene underneath, formed out of clay by Brigitte. All the families here got together recently for a song and celebration evening. Yesterday, a truck took us to a nativity play in Krusendorf, and later we celebrated Christmas Eve in our rooms. Today at noon, there was a feast with presents for the children, given by the very friendly English officers. Now we feel *gemütlich* here as a family. Papa has read to us about the life of Jesus here on earth, Ulrich is lying on his stomach on the carpet, building something with his new blocks, Brigitte is reading, and I'm writing. May the hope of salvation penetrate our thinking and help all hard-hit humanity to go forward with hope.

On the next page in the album, Klara had pasted a homemade calendar, Brigitte's gift to her at Christmas. It lists activities for the first five days of 1946: "On New Year's Day: Five o'clock Tea at Admiral Rhein's. On the 2nd: Sing-along Evening for Women. On the 3rd: Trip to Kiel to visit Frau Seemann and get some books, to visit Frl. Wienroth, and to see a tailor for some alterations."

New clothes were unobtainable at that time, and it required much creativity to alter the growing children's clothes to fit. Skirts and dresses often had a broad strip of fabric from another source inserted at the bottom. Boys' pants were lengthened with some useable cloth from worn-out men's pants.

"On the 4th: Trip to two villages, Surendorf and Krusendorf."

I suspect that these trips had as their objective buying some vegetables and perhaps meat, if available, from local farmers. Klara had to pay not only with money, but also with cigarettes and some valuables, such as cameras, watches, or jewelry.

"On the 5th: Invite the bachelors over for Tea. Also get the address of the doctor responsible for our area in Eckernförde."

The next entry by Klara into Brigitte's album is dated May 7, 1946.

> This may be the most wonderful spring that we have experienced in years, perhaps in our lifetimes. How full of terror was the springtime last year—how peaceful, by contrast, this year! However, the situation in the world, especially in our poor Deutschland, is still very sad. The condition of our people in the East, under Russian occupation, makes us all feel depressed since there seems to be no hope for them. And there are millions of homeless people on the streets and in the train stations, refugees looking for shelter. May God give them refuge and a bettering of their circumstances.
>
> Here in our blooming, woodsy surroundings, we pass the time working steadily, but with enough time for leisure. The early spring was glorious in this blessed portion of the country. Snowdrops in the woods, followed by a carpet of anemones. Now the forest is green—a miracle! The question at this time is what will happen with Papa's work. He'll probably soon continue to work in Kiel, but for how long?
>
> We pray every evening for God's protection. Brigitte doesn't go to school yet, but the private lessons will continue. She works avidly in the gardens, knits socks for herself, and helps everyone. Every day, she tutors her friends, Martin and Ute Hofer, with their homework, but afterward she squats like a three-year-old in front of the homemade dollhouse and plays with "family Puck." Movies are very popular with her and with Uli.

> The country is suffering from famine; it is desperate in the cities. We have a bit more to eat, but I have to go into the countryside every few days to try to obtain something extra from the farmers. It's good that Brigitte, at age thirteen, can now look out for Uli and the household. Yes, we now have a grown-up daughter! But she'll still be our little *Schnuppi* and honey.
>
> Gitte draws and paints with skill and enjoyment. She made me a Madonna painting for my little May altar. *(Klara had always continued some Catholic customs, like celebrating May first as the day of Mary, mother of Jesus Christ.)* Right now, both children are lying in bed but are allowed to read; that's a treat for them. Written in the Merry Month of May, 1946.

Klara added later, "Today, a few more words in this fairy-tale lovely May in Dänisch-Nienhof."

It's so clear to me, translating these notes, that a heavy weight of fear and responsibility had lifted from my mother's shoulders. She was finally free, after five and a half years of war, to take some deep breaths, look around at nature, and rejoice in just being alive in peacetime.

Klara continued:

> On Sunday, the nineteenth of May, exactly on Mother's Day, Brigitte had her first confirmation lesson. With this step, she begins her adulthood. And yet, it seems that she was just baptized! She will be fourteen on June 30, and this lesson is earlier than usual, but that's necessary because of our uncertainty in regard to our future. Pastor Hollstein gave her the first lesson in the chapel at Nienhof, following the service for adults in the afternoon. The trip on foot to Krusendorf is so far that Rev. Hollstein kindly agreed to teach Brigitte in this manner for now. He lent her a little catechism and a hymnbook.

> Just now, she planted the last beans in the garden. She's amazingly helpful in the garden. May God bless these earthly seeds, and also those that are being planted in this time of preparation in her soul.

I remember: The catechism was dry. I was learning the words, but they didn't touch my heart. Jesus said to love God like an abba, *a daddy, a loving father. But how could a loving father cause or tolerate such destruction as we had just lived through? And how could he demand that his son suffer through a terrible sacrifice? Even though Jesus prayed in the Garden of Gethsemane, "My Father, if it be possible, let this cup pass from me; nevertheless, not as I will, but as thou wilt," he had to go through with it. And then he had to endure false accusations, shame, beatings, wearing a crown of thorns, and carry his own heavy wooden cross up to the hill of Golgatha, be nailed to it, and die of exposure, trauma, and dehydration. The saddest event in the Bible, to me, is that Jesus died in despair, crying out with a loud voice, "My God, my God, why hast thou forsaken me?" I cannot feel close to a "father" who demands this.*

These questions have remained with me throughout my life and may color my remembrances somewhat in the way I've articulated them here. And yet, and yet—there is something mysterious and potent about a willing and accepting sacrifice. I cannot put my finger on what that signifies. Sacrifice, for the sake of others, is a powerful symbol in many religions and myths. It moves me; it touches something deep inside me.

Once, many years ago, our yellow cat Samson came in from the woods in a subdued mood. I picked him up and held him on my lap as I sat at the kitchen table looking out. Then I gently examined him and found a lemon-sized, tender mass on his belly, an abscess, perhaps from a fight. It was surely very painful. As I waited for someone to come home to watch my toddler so that I could take Samson to the vet, I continued to stroke Samson and he lay perfectly still, not making a sound or stirring. A strange sensation came over me. I felt that Samson was willingly taking on some suffering of the world, perhaps especially taking it away from our family. He was making a quiet sacrifice. That powerful feeling has never faded for me. I'm happy to report that Samson made a complete recovery.

As I am writing this, in my early seventies, I still puzzle over the Old Testament story in which God commands Abraham to sacrifice his son, Isaac. That's child abuse in my mind. What kind of loving God the Father demands that of a human father? And what kind of father takes his son out, binds him, lays him on the altar for a burnt offering, and raises his weapon, ready to kill him, because a voice in his head tells him to do this? Even though at the last minute "an angel" intervened, this story is gruesome. The terrible thing is that three religions—Judaism, Christianity, and Islam—revere Abraham for doing this in the name of obeying God. I do not understand it. I cannot relate to it. But I can see where the cruel and violent elements fostered by these religions originate. In addition, of course, there is the problem of Abraham's first son, Ishmael, who became inconvenient and was sent away to perish in the wilderness with his mother. But he but survived, and among his descendants was Mohammed. I believe that blind obedience to an evil command is never right. Just recently, I discussed this issue with several theologians. They explained that Abraham is revered not so much for having obeyed God's command as for having been chosen by God.

But this is a distant God, who does not intervene when horrible things happen to us humans fighting each other here on earth, as during the war. I consider myself a good mother and grandmother. If I see my children or grandchildren squabble, I do not let it get to the point of violence. I intervene. I may scold or punish, but most often I serve as a mediator, or teacher, on how to handle conflicts. That's what a good father or mother should do. If we lived in a world and with a religion in which women exerted more power and influence, then perhaps there will be hope for a better future for us on our planet.

I remember: I was now almost fourteen years old. I could pray more easily to Jesus, who spoke of love, than to God, the Father. But I didn't really deeply understand much of what I read in the Bible. I read the catechism and the Bible with the same interest, wonder, occasional revulsion, and yet detachment as I read myths and fairy tales. How could I believe that Jesus was resurrected from death? I was enough of a pragmatist, a realist, that it seemed unbelievable that after his death he came and talked to his disciples, his long-time friends, while they were walking on the road to Emmaus, and they saw him as an ordinary man and didn't recognize him until he had talked to them for quite a while. If he was resurrected, why did he look like someone else? Was this just a giant hoax? Why couldn't I feel comfortable discussing all this with Pastor Hollstein or my parents, rather than learning those dry, emotionless catechism routines? I guess I didn't want to show my lack of faith.

What a change from my intense faith of earlier years!

Klara wrote in Brigitte's album on July 7, 1946:

> Oh, what a nice a birthday we had on June 30 for our big daughter, now fourteen, and her brother on the same day, now ten! Papa had returned just the day before from the hospital in Kiel, where he had a successful hernia operation. And a few days before that, three cases of our books arrived, which we had stored in Bad Frankenhausen during our evacuation. Brigitte's beloved, familiar book friends were there: *Heidi* by Johanna Spyri and *The Wonderful Journey of the Wild Geese* by Selma Lagerlöf and so many others. Both kids got some of these as presents for the second time and were thrilled. The main birthday present for Brigitte, however, was . . . four healthy rabbits! Brigitte loves them and will have her hands full to feed them and care for them.

I myself wrote the next note into my album on September 9, 1946.

> Now I will write something myself in my album. It's Saturday afternoon, just after midday dinner. Later, I won't have any more time for writing. I'll have to clean out my rabbit hutches and straighten out our room. Then I have to do my homework, and then I'll help Ute and Martin Hofer with theirs. They are the

children of the next-door farmers. Even though Erdmute (Ute) is only eight years old, I like to play with her with my dollhouse. Puck, the man doll, will say to Pucki, the woman, "I love you so much." And while they're kissing, little Bobby climbs up on the roof and through the chimney he pulls up the pots that are cooking dinner on the hearth, and he eats up everything.

We often go looking for mushrooms in the woods. I know all the edible ones, big *Steinpilze* [boletus] and yellow crumpled *Pfifferlinge* [chanterelles]. The poisonous *Fliegenpilze* [toadstools] I avoid. They're easily recognized, red with white spots. Even though they are toxic, they're considered a symbol of good luck. Isn't that strange?

Since those days, I have never found any mushrooms with the wonderful taste of those wild ones I collected in Dänisch-Nienhof.

I also like to go out with a basket to pick raspberries and blackberries. I leave early in the morning, wearing a pretty dress that looks bit like a *Dirndl* [native dress, a jumper of blue-print cotton with a white, puffy, short-sleeved blouse underneath], and enjoy the sunshine, birdsong, solitude, crisp air, dew on the bushes, and ripe berries peeking out among the leaves.

Now I have to stop writing, or I won't finish with my rabbits. I have three brown ones, one black, and one gray. They have young ones frequently. I'll keep my old favorite pets, but of the others we'll eat one every Sunday. That's usually the only meat we'll have. I feed them hay, and I also let them out on the grass in back of the house. They love dandelion greens, plantains, clover, and other weeds and grass. [Next to my writing on the page, there's my drawing of two large rabbit hutches with their occupants, as well as a big woodpile.]

> I've watched Papa butcher rabbits, clean them, and then skin them. The fur will be made into muffs and hats.

All cooking by the three families in the women's barrack was done on a wood-burning stove. This stove was often quite temperamental and required loving care and attention. (*I don't recall how the women divided their kitchen time because I was never invited to help in the kitchen.*)

On January 15, 1947, I wrote the next entry in my album:

> Our Dänisch-Nienhof Christmas was again lovely. We heard Christmas music on the radio, and then Papa read us the Christmas gospel. Then finally we could go over to the sofa to see our presents. *Bang!* The lights went out, and there we sat in the dark. But Mutti lit a small candle and we could see a little. Then Papa found the petroleum lamp he had "appropriated" and so we could save our last candle.

The term organisieren *(appropriating) was used in Germany during and after the war to denote any way of getting something, whether by buying or bartering or "finding." It was used not in a derogatory sense, but with an air of admiration for someone who could cope.*

Going on in my album:

> I got a whole new outfit for Christmas: a skirt, a pullover, knee socks, a collar, a nightie, and a pair of pants. These pants have been made from a used uniform, and they're forest green in color. They fit quite snugly, and where my upper thighs don't quite touch because they're too skinny, there's a little space right at my crotch. It looks like a little hole. Somehow that makes me feel uncomfortable, as if it has a sexual connotation. [How interesting that in 2013, the "thigh gap" is considered fashionable.]
>
> Of course I received books, also. Without books, Christmas is unthinkable. Fortunately, the electricity returned soon, and Uli and I could lie on the floor and read. We also played a lot of card games. Papa and I had picked out our Christmas tree in the woods and we picked the prettiest one. On New Year's Eve, we stayed up 'til midnight. Mutti baked a carp, mmmm—*ganz prima* [first class]!
>
> We've had additions to our family. Two mother rabbits had young ones on the same day. One had five. Professor Wigge got two of them. The other had three black ones. They're my favorites. One always licks my hand; that tickles. The mother rabbit has a kind of beard under her chin. I laugh at her; she gets mad and runs into the corner. That reminds me: when I put a male in with the female, the female runs around and up into the hay trough as if she has no intention to mate. I wonder whether she is just playing hard to get or really doesn't like it. Now I'm going to finish here

> and go to the beach to see the icebergs in the ocean. *Tschüss* [Bye].

I remember: One day, someone arranged for a chess master to come and play against us. There were about eight of us sitting at two long tables, and the chess master went from one to the other. He was obviously very good, but I won against him. I was so proud!

January 1947 was cold, and food became even more scarce. *I remember this very well: All we ever had to eat was* Graupen *(barley) and* Rüben *(rutabaga). I was sick and tired of these. Sometimes, just for variety, the barley would have some little worms in it. Extra protein! Ugh! One day, there was an exciting rumor in the camp. A horse had stepped on a live wire in a field not far away and was electrocuted. All available adults got knives and pots and ran to the scene. We children ran, too. And there it was! A brown horse that looked quite young and healthy, lying on its side on the ground. After the men had cautiously removed the wires, everyone cut off all the meat they could carry. That meat made wonderful roasts and stews! It was delicious. Much better than rabbit meat.*

I also can picture another occasion clearly in my mind: An elegant lady visited us. I don't remember the context of the visit, only that she looked at me with approbation and commented on my "beautiful, ash-blond hair." It was my first real, direct compliment, and meant a lot to me. Mutti didn't often look at me in a proud, approving way, as I saw other mothers do with their children. She had a habit, especially when others were present, to shake her head in a negative kind of way when I was present. In retrospect, I wonder whether it was her way of appearing humble. Or maybe it was her way of averting the evil eye, as Mediterranean people do.

Entry by Klara into Brigitte's album, dated February 15, 1947: "Here's a photo of our family on our sofa. Soon we'll be separated from our Papa again, probably for quite some time. Erich will move to America in the next few weeks, and we won't follow for months. It's another chapter in our turbulent lives. May this fateful and meaningful step be blessed. The situation here in our poor fatherland is hopeless and dim. Thousands are dying of starvation and cold. The economic future looks bad for the foreseeable future. Therefore, we must be grateful to have been given this chance. We will try to see the best side of our new situation. We'll never forget our dear Dänisch-Nienhof, the beautiful forest and trails, and ocean view."

I don't remember any discussion about this momentous decision at all, either overhearing the adults talking or involving us children!

Klara continued her writing: "Next Saturday, Brigitte will have her Confirmation. That's a big step in her young life. May God give his blessings."

On the next page of the album, there are telegrams. "Best wishes and congratulations on the Confirmation from Oma and all the others in Voerde"; "On your Confirmation our warmest wishes from Tante Johanna and Onkel Toni Bochem," from Düsseldorf. Klara also had pasted in a branch of boxwood from the Confirmation table.

Klara wrote a typewritten letter to family and friends and pasted a copy in Brigitte's album:

Dänisch-Nienhof, February 24, 1947
Dear Loved Ones,

I've just cleared some space on the desk for my typewriter, with difficulty. That's because it is Brigitte's Confirmation table and it is still covered with a white tablecloth and decorated with boxwood branches. The candelabrum is still standing there and all the little gifts lie around it.

Now I'll tell you a little about how the twenty-second of February passed. To make it simpler (or out of laziness) I'm making several copies. I'll do like this in the future also, whenever more detailed descriptions of our life are indicated, which I can do enthusiastically once, but less so several times.

Reading this, I truly appreciate today's computers and printers.

We're quite happy to have advanced Brigitte's Confirmation, since the usual age is fifteen. In this way, we could celebrate in peace and quiet. We're sitting here in uncertainty since we don't know the date of our departure to another town, nor of Erich's ship to America. The telegram could arrive any day, or be delayed for a long time.

On Saturday morning, all of us, including the other occupants of the house, worked hard to arrange the room. Tables and furniture were moved around. Papa had to open the bottom-most packing box in the attic, and for the first time in many years, we took out damask tablecloths and the good silver. The desk became an altar and three tables were set for eighteen people. Actually four more arrived later, so that we were twenty-two. In these days, that can be quite a problem in regard to food, but thanks to farmers in the neighborhood and to friends, it all worked out.

Typical for the times, a dress and shoes did not arrive until just before the ceremony. Our own little family of four had lunch. One of the rabbits had to give its all. Then, at one o'clock, the guests started arriving: the Schwennesens and the Pfitzmanns from Kiel; our four housemates—the Rahlfs and Neumanns; Mr. Sorensen, Papa's colleague from the camp; as well as Professor Wigge, the Hofers, and Pastor Hollstein. The pastor brought some little hymnbooks and we sang "God Has Brought Me Here" and several others. Brigitte had already had her examination during her last lesson. Then came a short sermon on Brigitte's Confirmation theme, "I am the way, the truth, and the life; no one comes to the Father, but through me" (John 14:6). It was remarkable that even those guests who are not very religious followed the proceedings with great interest. Another hymn followed and then the Apostles' Creed, spoken by everyone. Now Brigitte had to complete the ceremony by expounding on Martin Luther's explanation of the second article. I was full of anxiety, but all went well.

Brigitte knelt and was given the blessing and received into the church. Another hymn followed, *"So nimm denn meine Hände und führe mich"* [Take My Hands and Guide Me].

And in this way, Brigitte became a member of the Christian church and a *Weltanschauung* [view of the world] which we have strived to provide in our home. We hope sincerely that what she has received will help her through many difficulties and doubts and through many questions of existence.

It is remarkable, I think, that I remember almost nothing about this event, certainly nothing spiritual. It seems to have been more important for the adults than for me.

The spiritual mood became one of more earthly pleasures as the aroma of real coffee filled the room. And then sixteen cakes arrived in merry procession, from tortes to simple honey cakes. Every guest had contributed something. Later on, we also had some small sandwiches, very tasty after all the sweet stuff. These were accompanied by a real man's *Kümmel* [caraway liqueur]. The women didn't decline it, either. There were only six liqueur glasses; they were passed around. The pastor, a fairly young man, participated vigorously in all these worldly pleasures. He then intoned some folksongs, and we all joined in happily and loudly. Papa gave a little talk, during which there were some tears when he spoke of goodbyes and uncertain futures, of separation and reunion.

Afterward, Dr. Wigge organized some games, and spirits rose again. Brigitte enjoyed her gifts, especially the watch and books.

I remember primarily a little rosewood box, containing a travel chess set, which I treasured for years. I also remember that Mutti didn't seem to like the pastor's selection of my Confirmation theme very much. I think she'd have preferred something about guardian angels. It is noteworthy how lovingly my mother described the rare occasions when food was abundant during this postwar period of semifamine.

Our celebration continued the next day with leftovers and games.

Now, on the twenty-third of February 1946, we're quite snowed in and wonder what awaits us in the future. During this week, we still have to do a large laundry and then we have to process, by boiling, a huge quantity of sugar beets for sugar. However, I hope to escape that dreadful chore by giving the beets to a neighbor, who may then keep half of the proceeds.

We'll be moving to Landshut, in Bavaria, where we'll be living in an apartment complex until we can go to America to join Erich. I have heard that there will be ample food provisions there and so it's all right to give some away now. Tomorrow we'll start packing some boxes and suitcases for Erich. And now, we'll go out for a little walk in the deep snow. Our love and warmest wishes to all,

Klara, Erich, Brigitte, and Ulrich

CHAPTER 13

Erich's documents, 1946–1969: Denazification, immigration, navy contracts.

As I am beginning to write this chapter in 2006, and revising it in 2014 at age eighty-one, I am grateful for the extensive amount of source material that I have had to work with.

Rummaging through many boxes of letters, documents, diaries, books, interviews, and photo albums, I came upon several most interesting folders, which my father Erich had saved. They represent the time just after the war and are quite enlightening from a historical point of view. Erich was a very organized person, congruent with his profession as physicist, and kept detailed records. My mother, Klara, wrote diaries, articles, and photo albums with much commentary. It is somewhat miraculous that all these documents survived our family evacuations and moves during the war and after emigration to the United States of America.

The folders I discovered deal with "denazification" testimonials, immigration forms, a two-inch folder of letters to city hall, offices, lawyers, and other persons in the attempt to recover my parents' furniture and rental title to their apartment in Berlin-Spandau (then in the Russian-occupied sector), Erich's publications and patents, and his early and later contracts with the US Navy. I have translated excerpts of these items, not necessarily always in chronological order. I realize that there are too many details, sometimes confusing, and that I might have condensed them even more. However, I decided to keep this chapter intact as a good example of the bureaucracy and disorder of those postwar years.

"DENAZIFICATION" DOCUMENTS

My father wrote a brief curriculum vitae *(résumé) while in Dänisch-Nienhof on October 10, 1946. This and the following items apparently were in answer to questions that led to his "denazification" clearance.*

After their victory, the Allies instituted a general program of removing Nazi party members, who had been persons of influence, from office. Also, the swastika was removed from public places.

Germans had to fill out forms even if they, like my father and mother, had not been members of the National Socialist German Workers party. The United States and Great Britain also initiated a successful campaign, which induced among Germans a feeling of collective guilt for the war and for civil and war crimes. They did this by publishing German atrocities extensively while minimizing those committed by the Allies, not only the Russians, but also British and Americans, such as the 14 million Germans displaced from the East, the millions who died in Russian gulags, and the civilians killed by bombs. While such propaganda is not unusual for the victors of a war or conflict, the horrors of the Holocaust in the concentration camps were unprecedented, of course. Germany and Germans have carried the burden of guilt, have paid reparations, and are still haunted by the question of how something dreadful like this could have happened.

In his CV (*curriculum vitae*), after noting his earlier studies and work, Erich wrote:

> On November 11, 1929, I started as physicist in the CPVA [Chemistry and Physics Research Station] of the navy. I worked with infrared radiation, compression tolerance of materials, underwater vibrations, physics of explosives, etc. The results were considered classified at the time. In 1934, I became director of the physics division. In 1937, I edited the textbook on explosives studies.
>
> On December 12, 1939, I was commanded to the OKM [*Oberkommando der Marine*, high command of the navy] in Berlin, and my duties were to lead the navy's research activities. After the capitulation, I was appointed, by the occupying forces, director of the CPVA, with the objective to make reports to the

> [British] Royal Navy and to bring to a conclusion previously begun research studies.

Erich listed a secret German patent granted in 1940—Explosive Shells with Incendiary Effect—and another—Bottom Mine Having a Shock Wave Effect in a Desired Direction, a secret German patent granted in 1944. The first patent was adapted for use in submarine ammunition. Both patents were claimed by the navy. A list of publications itemizes fourteen papers, dealing mostly with underwater explosives.

Next, Erich needed to provide testimonials of five reliable persons, well acquainted socially and professionally with him and with Klara. He gave a list of seven, including colleagues, two ministers, and the family physician. Their testimonies, signed under oath, are in the folder. Most state that they knew Erich and Klara for a lengthy period of time, that the Buchmanns were exemplary colleagues/parents/neighbors, and that they were not members of the NSDAP (National Social German Workers Party, a.k.a. Nazis). Here are a few examples:

"Herewith I declare under oath that I know Mrs. Klara Buchmann and her daughter, Brigitte, presently in Landshut, for a long time, dating back to Berlin, 1940–44. I was often in their home. Their marriage and family life are known to me to be harmonious. As far as I know, Mrs. Klara Buchmann never belonged to the party nor the *Frauenschaft* [Women's Organization]. She was in opposition to the *Zeitgeist* [political currents of the time], which was in harmony with my own feelings. The family's social life was active and in correspondence with their high cultural standards. Relations with neighbors were without problems. I myself never belonged to the NSDAP and I am not related to the Buchmanns. Isabella Beutlich, March 6, 1948."

"I was the personal physician of the family of Dr. Erich Buchmann for many years, which gave me the opportunity to determine the spirit of the household. I'm under the impression that the developments of the regime at that time went against

Erich's inner beliefs. I myself was not a member of the party. Dr. Sasse."

"I've known Director Dr. Erich Buchmann since he started working at the CPVA in 1929 and can give a testimonial regarding his political beliefs. Dr. Buchmann knew that I had been a member of the SPD [*Sozialdemokratische Partei Deutschlands,* Social Democratic Party of Germany (one of six parties at that time, a Marxist party)] since 1910 and never joined the NSDAP. However, Dr. B. always stood by me and made sure that I would not be dismissed despite my political leanings. In one case, it is thanks to him that I was not incarcerated in a concentration camp. I had allowed my son to enter the *Kampfsportverband* [Martial Arts Alliance]. (*All sports groups, such as bicycle or hiking groups, were discouraged under Hitler, who instead promoted membership in the Hitler Youth.*) This was not allowed by our work rules. I was secretly reported; and since I had been warned several times previously, I was to be deported to a concentration camp. However, Dr. Buchmann intervened and saved me from this. Dr. B. was known by his colleagues and subordinates for his unsympathetic position in regard to the party. (Signed) Lammers, Dänisch-Nienhof, March 1, 1947."

LETTERS, 1945–51, ABOUT THE ENORMOUS EFFORTS TO RETAIN THE BERLIN APARTMENT, FURNITURE, ART, BOOKS, BANK ACCOUNTS, ETC.

The next folder, very thick, deals with my parents' attempts to safeguard their Berlin possessions. As we can imagine, conditions in Germany during and after the war were chaotic. I was amazed to find this huge folder of correspondence to various officials, attempting to retain their title to the Berlin apartment, and to obtain their furniture. This correspondence began postwar in 1945 (while we were in Dänisch-Nienhof), continued into 1947 (while we were in Landshut), and partly continued even into 1951, years after we had moved to the United States. Most of the correspondence is typewritten, with carbon copies in the folder of my father's answers. Notes are sometimes jotted down on the back of old technical pages, due to the paper shortage of the time. There are also many handwritten letters on fragile, yellowed paper with faded ink, and even postcards.

Among the interesting information is a handwritten listing of bank accounts in the *Sparkasse der Stadt Berlin* (Savings Bank of the City of Berlin). The amounts are in RMk (*Reichsmarks*). The equivalent value in dollars, at that time, was approximately 1 RM to $4. There were accounts in Erich's name (5,479), Klara's (3,213), Brigitte's (601) and Ulrich's (576). Also, "new" accounts (2,150 and 2,500). The total was equivalent to about five to six years of salary, quite a bit of money, some of which had been earmarked for a new Volkswagen. Unfortunately, the Russians expropriated all this.

In regard to the furniture, the first document is a long, handwritten letter by Isabella Beutlich to Klara, difficult to read at this time. She wrote from Berlin-Spandau, on December 2, 1945.

> Today, one year ago, we celebrated the first day of Advent together with you [in Berlin], and now I'm constantly thinking of you. I just listened to Christmas carols on the radio, which a friend lent me, for a few hours. [!] We wish we could forget the bad times, but they are still frighteningly close. I'm happy to hear that you four are reunited. I had written you in Frankenhausen during the summer, but apparently the letter didn't get there in time. I'll tell you about some of the troubles with your apartment.

I'll now summarize:

> During the fighting in Berlin [in the last days of the war], I couldn't get there. Those days were terrifying. Heavy artillery stood in front of our house, and when Berlin was occupied, we were thrown out of our home

> by the Russians. I packed some suitcases, put them into a little wagon, and had to leave on foot.

Mrs. Beutlich found shelter with two women in another part of Berlin. She described the desperate food shortage (only four heads of cabbage as the only vegetable since April!) in great detail.

> In regard to your apartment, there was a mortar shell that directly hit your dining room during the last days of the war. It shattered the glass door and went through the bathroom into the pantry. A family of eight bombed-out refugees had been assigned to the apartment. They threw all your books on the floor, broke open the desk drawers, and left some photo albums, which you had so lovingly prepared, in disarray. The large Oriental rug is gone, as well as some furniture. In the cellar storage area, there are still some boxes. I think the one with porcelain is intact. I've taken a large carton of books. A neighbor took your sewing machine, to keep it safe, and the radio and round table. Your brother-in-law [Kurt, Erich's younger brother, who lived in another section of Berlin at the time] came after some months, but he hasn't gone to the district office yet. His wife [Maria] took some baby things and curtain material and books.

An official notification is next in the folder, from the Spandau District of Berlin, dated January 1, 1946, and stating that all possessions were under protection of their office. The current renter, Herr Hans Schmidt, was to be responsible for all furniture and other items. All items would be released to Dr. Erich Buchmann upon his return to Berlin.

A neighbor described in a letter that Herr Schmidt had nailed plywood over the broken windows and stored the Buchmann furniture in the unheated rooms.

On November 24, 1945, Herr Schmidt wrote under the letterhead "Hans Schmidt—Wholesale Dealer in Vegetables and Fruit, Spandau." He stated that the Buchmann furniture was under official safeguard. He himself was using the kitchen and the *Bauernzimmer* (dining alcove in rustic style). He couldn't release anything, not even to Erich's brother.

Erich answered on May 20, 1946, that he could not come to Berlin. Apparently, the British officers would not give him, or Klara, permission to go into the Russian sector because of the danger of kidnapping of German scientists by the Russians. Several scientists and their families had been "snatched." Berlin at this time was located like an isolated pearl in Soviet-occupied Germany, which later became communist East Germany. The city, being the capital, was divided by the occupying forces into four sectors, just like the country—American, British, French, and Soviet.

Erich asked for a rental fee to be paid by Herr Schmidt for the furniture he was using. Also, he wrote, there was now a release from the previous protection order. Herr Schmidt answered that he'd be willing to buy all the furniture and asked for a price. Erich wrote that he needed all his furniture urgently for his own family.

Next in the folder is a letter to a Herr Laubach, who apparently had removed the beautiful bedroom set and moved it into his own apartment. "We understand that you are using our walnut bedroom suite. You may continue to do so, paying a rental fee of M 5.00/month, payable to Dr. Kurt Buchmann." Laubach's answer was that the bedroom set had been infested with lice and moths and required four men for the cleaning. After all that work, he was not willing to pay a rental fee.

Now Erich wrote to the rental office of Spandau and several other types of "city hall" offices. Even the British camp commander wrote. But it was apparent that already there was friction, later leading to the Cold War, between the different occupying forces. Finally, one bureaucrat recommended a lawyer.

In September 1946, Maria, Kurt's wife, sent a letter saying that the two damaged front rooms had been repaired enough to allow two women to live there with their children. "They're not the best renters; they have soldiers visiting." In the meantime, Erich had hired a lawyer in Berlin, a Herr Willi Missmann.

Now there was a (funny to me) letter from Hans Schmidt. He stated that he didn't care why Erich left Berlin and why he couldn't return. He, Hans, was paying the rent, and considered himself the official renter. Also he refused to pay rent for furniture use, and on the contrary, wanted to charge Erich for taking care of his possessions! The correspondence continued back and forth, back and forth.

I saw, in the folder, a copy of an extensive inventory of ownership, made out originally by Erich and Klara in June 1943. The inventory lists, in great detail, not only furniture but art work, the piano, clothing, linens, silver, radio, record player, porcelain, and jewelry. The books alone totaled 534 in number, valued at approximately RM 2,000 ($ 8,000) at that time. (*At that time, a two-bedroom house in the United States could be bought for $3,000.*)

In January, 1947, Erich wrote his brother Kurt in Berlin that the British commander of the camp in Dänisch-Nienhof had agreed to send one of his officers and a truck to pick up Erich's possessions. Apparently that didn't happen, though, because the next letter by Erich, on February 2, 1947, stated that he had just signed a contract with the American Navy and that he and his family would move to Landshut, in Bavaria, awaiting transport to the United States. Now he was counting on the Americans to pick up the furniture and bring it to Landshut.

A new snag: According to a new German law, No. 52, Erich was not supposed to be able to keep his furniture because he was a Ministerialrat under the Hitler regime. More back and forth, proving that this law did not apply to Erich because he was not a party member.

A telegram from Kurt, in Berlin, to Klara, who was now in Landshut, on April 20, 1947: "Let us know immediately when the truck for the furniture is arriving, since we're planning a vacation into the West on May first."

In May, Erich wrote to a Captain Hirsch about the truck. But nothing happened.

On June 28, 1947, a very irritated Kurt wrote to Klara in Landshut that nothing was happening and he was sick and tired of always waiting and being ready, and not getting any appreciation from her or his brother Erich, who was in the United States by now.

And next there follows a new complication: On June 14, the district office of the ODF (*Opfer des Faschismus*, victims of fascism) wrote to the lawyer, Herr Missmann, regarding the bedroom suite. "Herr Löbel is a recognized ODF. He has lost, through the people who belonged to the NSDAP, everything he owned. If he now has to give up the bedroom suite, he will again have nothing. In addition, his wife is expecting a baby any day now. We find it brazen that you are writing about a rental fee. Who asked, for the last twelve and a half years, about the Jews and anti-fascists, from whom everything was taken, who were incarcerated without trial, murdered in the most brutal way? Who gives the fathers back to the children, the breadwinners to the wives, and the sons and daughters to their parents? No one, Herr Missmann. Dr. Buchmann can sue us about his furniture, because we cannot ask any ODF to be without furniture for his family."

On July 13, Klara wrote to Kurt that Captain Hirsch would pick up the furniture very soon. In regard to the bedroom suite, she said that it had best be picked up at the same time, but if that wasn't possible, then Herr Missmann would pursue the matter later.

The correspondence continued in regard to the bedroom suite, with multiple offices again involved.

On November 11, 1947, Klara wrote a letter of thanks to Captain Hirsch for bringing the furniture to Landshut. It had finally arrived in October. She asked him to continue to try to obtain the bedroom suite, since it could be well used by one of Erich's three bombed-out brothers.

The next letter in the file is a copy of Erich's request, now written from the United States to the District Office Spandau to release the bedroom furniture. It is dated September 30, 1949.

On November 26, 1950, Erich wrote to Herr Löbel that he had gotten his letter of January 9, 1950, and would sell him the bedroom suite for DM 175. On April 1, 1951, he wrote him again. After that, there are no more copies of any letters in the file.

Whew! Just looking through this file and translating it, I am exhausted. Furniture of the quality of that of my parents' was a valuable commodity and nothing could be obtained during the war and in the years afterward, when all major cities were 50 to 80 percent destroyed, including factories. Everyone was in great need. How difficult it all was during that time!

I remember some of these items in our house in the United States: the piano, Papa's large wooden desk, rose-upholstered sofa and armchairs, paintings, probably some linens, Mutti's silver, some books.

IMMIGRATION DOCUMENTS, 1947, AND CONTRACTS, 1947–69

The next three folders contain fascinating, sometimes "restricted" or "secret," documents relating to Erich's contracts with the United States and immigration details. Erich signed a "Special Contract for Employment of German Nationals with the War Department in the United States" on February 6, 1947, while he was working for the British Royal Navy in Dänisch-Nienhof after the war. The new contract with the United States called for a six-month minimum period, with a salary of approximately $12,000 a year.

It is astonishing to me how quickly German scientists came under protective custody by the occupying forces and how vigorously the American and Soviet governments competed for them. England and France apparently didn't have the funds and facilities to offer much. We are all familiar with Wernher von Braun and his rocket scientists, but there obviously were other specialties, such as that of my father, which were in demand.

Another document by Lieutenant Commander, Royal Navy, J. Morgan went to the German naval control officer in Kiel on February 10: "Request *Marinebaudirektor* [Navy Construction Director] Dr. Erich Buchmann may be given a priority discharge.

He is under contract for civil employment with the American authorities and has been vetted by the British authorities both in England and Germany."

The next two-page typed document is marked "Restricted" on top. The letterhead is Headquarters US Forces, European Theater, and the date is March 13, 1947. Subject: Project "Paperclip."

I will summarize: The purpose of this directive is to set forth the responsibilities for the shipment of approximately 721 German and Austrian specialists and approximately 1,000 families to the United States.

> . . . to make their knowledge and abilities available to our country. . . . Security—every effort will be made to prevent this operation from being publicized [!] . . . The housing area at Landshut, Bavaria, is to be set up as an assembly area . . . [Then follow a lot of details as to transportation, etc.]

On March 24, the T-Force naval liaison, Kiel, *Kriegsmarinearsenal* (war navy arsenal), wrote to Erich, "This is to certify that you have been contracted by the United States authorities and you will be evacuated . . . as early as possible. . . . You will apply for permits, ration cards, etc., to the German authorities in the usual manner . . . have everything prepared for a quick departure."

The following memo tickles my funny bone. It is a two-page, single-spaced missive stamped SECRET in red on top.

> From: Lieutenant P. Jordan, RNVR, T-Force Naval Liaison, c/o SDO, Senior Naval Officer Schleswig-Holstein.
> Date: March 29, 1947.
> To: Lt. Welsh, Landshut Housing Project.
> Copies to: Naval Technical Unit Europe, Office of Naval Advisor, OMGUS, Berlin.

There were others copied in, including my father. I'll summarize the memo's complaints.

> With regard to the evacuation of scientists being undertaken from this area under your charge, you are hereby informed of the following: (a) The truck you left at Dänisch-Nienhof to pick up family and belongings of Dr. Buchmann will not even carry their belongings, let alone the four persons concerned and your driver. . . . (b) It is considered a rather slipshod way to arrange these things. . . . (c) Despite the fact that British authorities—particularly this unit—are willing to help in every way on these operations, it happens time and again that evacuation parties turn up and suddenly remove people without telling either British or local German authorities, etc., with insufficient space and very vague arrangements.

Next, Lt. Jordan complained that Lt. Welsh didn't introduce himself, but just appeared with his drivers at their mess, expecting to eat there, without even the courtesy of a phone call. There are more complaints that follow, but this excerpt gives the gist of the memo.

On November 17, 1947, after the "Paperclip" contract expired, Erich signed a one-year "Contract for Employment of Foreign Nationals with the Navy Department of the United States," at the rate of $20 per day, as "physicist consultant on underwater explosion research including participation in program planning, theoretical work, and field experiments of a highly specialized nature." He was now working in the United States for the navy.

On December 31, 1947, Erich wrote the director of the David Taylor Model Basin, Carderock, Maryland, with a request for transportation of his family from Landshut to the United States. He mentioned that he had just taken a lease on a house in nearby Cabin John, Maryland. The request was granted, but it would take months until we finally arrived there. (*Erich later bought the two-bedroom, two-story house for approximately $3,000. And he sold it, with additions and* *improvements, in 1991 for approximately $ 300,000 when he and Klara moved to Atlanta to be close to me, my husband, and three grandchildren.)*

From then on, according to a multitude of contracts in the folder, there was a steady progression in title and compensation. By 1950, Erich was "Supervisory Physicist (Mechanics)" at a GS rating of 1310, and in 1960 he was GS 1310-13 at $11,935 per year, then in 1964, GS 1310-14/03 at $14,515.

On August 19, 1969, there was a memo:

> From: Chief of Naval Operations
> To: Commander, Naval Ship Research and Development Center, Washington, DC
> Subject: US Representation at NATO Naval Armaments Group Meeting, IEG/6 (SG/1)
>
> 1. It is requested that the services of Dr. Erich Buchmann, Head, Structural Vibrations Branch, be made available to represent the United States at the forthcoming meeting . . .

I will now summarize:

> 2. The meeting is to be held in Dunfermline, Scotland, UK, at the Naval Construction Research Establishment on 7 and 8 October 1969 . . .
> 3. Dr. Buchmann's past representation of the United States in this Sub Group has been remarkably effective and productive. His attendance at the October meeting will ensure the continuity of expertise and scientific competence considered essential for this meeting.

This chapter summarized the information in the folders I discovered.

CHAPTER 14

1947: Waiting in Landshut, Bavaria, to leave for the USA. Brigitte discovers boys.

Klara's next entry in Brigitte's photo/life album is dated Easter 1947. Klara was now forty-four years old and Erich was forty-one.

Landshut/Bavaria, Ostendstrasse 4b

We're in a new chapter of our lives again! By the end of this month, our Papa will probably be on a ship to America. And after a while, we'll see whether and when we will follow him. It was a big final rush to get everything packed up in Dänisch-Nienhof, and then it was a hectic, four-day, eventful journey to finally get here. Now we're busy getting settled into our next short-term home in an apartment complex. We spent four uncomfortable days in a guesthouse, but yesterday we moved into our own little apartment. Everything is very makeshift at this time. Our truck with furniture and household items hasn't arrived yet, so that we don't have even the basic necessities. But after the horrible war, one hardly notices such things.

And yet—we long for a feeling of being settled, of putting down roots, after moving so many times in the last few years.

Now we'll be separated from our Papa again, for a lengthy time, and then we'll see about following him into the New World or not!

It's a bitter thought to have to leave our homeland in order to build a new existence, to have food and shelter. Our poor Germany is too small for so many people, after absorbing the thousands of refugees from the East. And all these refugees came with nothing into largely destroyed cities.

We will try to preserve a bit of Deutschland in our next home in America and keep it for our children. But at the same time, we'll try with goodwill to understand the new culture and way of life and to accommodate to it as much as possible.

Especially today, at Easter, we beg God for his blessing on our new adventure!

Again, I am struck by the gutsy, brave attitude of my parents. They truly represent the pioneer spirit of people who came to America because they lived under circumstances in history when they wanted better opportunities for themselves and their children. They made the United States the country of freedom, of enterprise, of hard work, and of a willing and adventurous spirit. I am proud to be a first-generation immigrant along with them and my brother.

Erich wrote the next entry in Brigitte's album:

Landshut, May 8, 1947
Dear Brigitte,

Now, for the first time, I will write something in your album, which has become a "book of life" for you. I'll start with this quote: "Wie nützlich ist der kleinste Kreis, wenn mann ihn recht zu pflegen weiss" [Even the smallest group is helpful, if you know how to care for it]. We've been with many different small groups because the waves of fate have pushed us here and there. But everywhere we found that we could learn something, everywhere there were worthy people who could give us something of value. And we mustn't forget that everywhere there is our caring Father in heaven who will take you into his arms during the time of our separation.

> I'll include you in my prayers, and I hope you won't forget me. Perhaps I can nudge your memory from time to time with some packages of goodies. Stay well and happy!
>
> Your Papa

Erich left on May 13, 1947, from Bremerhaven on the twenty-thousand-ton American steamship *USS Holbrook.* He arrived in New York on May 24 and was then driven to Washington, DC. His new research involved studies on underwater vibrations and explosions, just as it had in Germany. He now worked for the US Navy, just as he had done for the German Navy, and even briefly for the Royal Navy previously. His research was classified, just as it had been before. He worked at the David Taylor Model Basin in Carderock, Maryland, a naval research station in a suburb of Washington, DC, which included an extensive complex of offices, laboratories, and wind tunnels.

I wish I had thought to ask my father how the American, British, and Soviet occupying forces knew about the German researchers, their work, and their locations after the war. The French apparently did not compete in offering positions. I also wish I could have discussed with him how he was able to switch to English for the scientific terms he had to use at work and for his needs in daily life. How long did it take, how difficult was it, did he have help? When we arrived in the States a year later, there wasn't anything like the ESL (English as a Second Language) classes that are offered in all schools and many community organizations now.

Erich wrote his family in Germany frequently and also often sent little packages of food and luxuries, like Crisco shortening or other fats, canned meat, chocolate, coffee, nylons, and pens.

Elsewhere in the world, in 1947, there were some significant developments. In the United States, Jackie Robinson broke the racial color line as a Brooklyn Dodger. On June 5, the secretary of state, George F. Marshall, spoke to Harvard students and proposed a comprehensive plan of aid to rebuild Europe. Twenty-five billion dollars were allocated to Europe; three-point-six billion dollars were given to Germany over the next ten years. The

Marshall Plan was also extended to Japan later. It made a huge difference in rebuilding these countries and their economies.

These numbers seem so small when compared with the Stimulus Package of seven hundred eighty-seven billion dollars passed by the US Congress in 2009 to help avoid a severe depression in the United States.

Another event happened in 1947: André Nahmias, my future husband-to-be, a Sephardic Jew from Alexandria, Egypt, arrived to study at the University of Texas in Austin.

In 1947, the Cold War had begun, with intense competition between democracy, freedom, and capitalism in the American sphere and Communist ideals and economy in the Soviet sphere of influence, including East Germany. Senator Joseph McCarthy, a Republican from Wisconsin, pursued a public policy of exposing alleged Communist and Soviet supporters and spies. The Rosenbergs and Alger Hiss were convicted and executed. (*Their guilt was confirmed by the recent opening of Russian documents.*) McCarthy's Senate hearings were playing on television sets in most homes in the states. They resulted in blacklists for Hollywood writers and actors, dismissals of some government employees, and harassment of some university professors. This oppressive policy continued for a decade. President Harry Truman's loyalty oath requirement for government employees made extensive background checks necessary. It has been said that in the Cold War, security trumped democratic freedom. (*And, to some extent, the same policy arose post-9/11.*)

On August 15, India's Jawaharlal Nehru declared independence from Britain. India and Pakistan became separate independent states. Nehru was a friend of Lord Mountbatten (*whose original German name was Battenberg*), who helped expedite the process.

Klara wrote in Brigitte's album on July 4, 1947:

> It's summer already! Papa's letters from the other side of the globe are fascinating. Compared to the situation here in our poor Germany, conditions of life and working overseas sound like a fairy tale. We hope

that everything continues to go well and pray for our faraway Papa every evening. The children are always astonished that when it's six o'clock in the evening here, it's only noon for Papa.

Birthdays were lovely for the children again. Brigitte has really shot up. Now, at fifteen as of four days ago, she is tall and thin. Perhaps she has grown too rapidly for her heart; I have to make sure she doesn't overdo it.

I remember Mutti taking me to a doctor, but I don't remember why. The physician listened to my chest and said that I had a heart murmur and might have an abnormal heart valve, perhaps as a consequence of the scarlet fever I had contracted at age ten. He then looked at my chest with a fluoroscope and said my heart was normal in size. I was very impressed by the doctor in his white coat and I know that Mutti was, too. In retrospect, I think that I probably had a benign murmur, common in childhood. But the doctor's statement caused my mother to worry about my heart from that moment on, and of course that probably worried me, too, although I wasn't conscious of it. Mutti didn't want me to overexert myself and often warned me about that. This focus on my heart may be the reason I've had episodes of PAT (paroxysmal atrial tachycardia) since childhood. Every so often, for no obvious reason, I become aware of a very rapid heartbeat; it may be 150 to 160 beats per minute. I learned early on that I could stop it by taking a deep breath, holding it, and pushing with my stomach muscles. Much later I learned that I was doing the "Valsalva maneuver," which slows the heartbeat by stimulating the vagus nerve. It wasn't until I was in my forties, overloaded with patients at work, children at home, house, yard, and social obligations, that I suspected that my PAT was often a response to an underlying, unexpressed anxiety. I still have these episodes; they increased dramatically when my second husband became frail, ill, and also ill tempered, and I was stressed by caregiving; and they decreased when he moved into a senior facility.

There are no more photos from Germany in my photo album. (*I suspect that all our cameras had been traded for food by then.*)

Now that the long and dreadful war was over, the overwhelming sentiment among Germans was relief. For years, the primary objective for everyone had been survival. It was a daily struggle to obtain enough food. That, unfortunately, was still a priority after the war. However, the air raids had stopped. In order to stay alive during the frequent bombing attacks, it had been necessary to be partially dressed every night, even in bed, and to have a suitcase packed. When the alarm siren sounded, it meant getting up and trudging down into the shelter. After the "all clear" sounded, we went up to see if our apartment was still there. And then we tried to get a little more sleep. This constant, daily stress went on week after week, month after month, year after year in most large cities. And now it was finally over!

I remember that it felt so luxurious and free to finally be able to sleep with bare feet. I used to hate to sleep in my clothes, especially those scratchy woolen stockings I had to wear every night. Even now, in my seventies, sixty years after the air raids, I still revel in the "free feet" feeling! Another sensation is left over from those childhood war years: occasionally, when I take a shower, a thought pops up as I apply shampoo: I'd better hurry; it would be bad if the siren would go off now. *As I rinse off, I might think,* Good, now at least I'm clean if the siren starts.

We had regular classes again, not in school, but in our apartment complex. A middle-aged woman teacher, who was in our group of people waiting to move overseas, was doing German with us, as well as geography, math, and basic physics. A younger, thin woman was teaching us English. We were reading Treasure Island. *That was a little difficult and it was British Oxford English. I wished we were learning American English. Another teacher, a nice man, was teaching Latin and botany.*

I have found some composition booklets from that time, stapled together out of old scrap paper, which my mother saved for me. My German essays are so mature and well written that I'm astounded at my young self! I have often thought that we're probably at our best intellectually from age ten to twenty. I remember just absorbing knowledge like a sponge.

There was a boy in my German class who was really cute. His name was Hartmut. He had smooth, tanned, long legs, light-brown hair with a wave, and blue eyes. One day I was looking at him sideways as he was sitting in class. He was wearing shorts, and I saw a bit of his pink scrotum peeking out! I admired his handwriting and tried to imitate it.

Two sisters were also in my class, even though they weren't the same age. The older was Ilse and the younger was Elli, who was prettier and also more fun.

I remember a particular event and wrote about it in my diary: "We went on a school trip to go swimming the other day. We sat in an army transport truck with long benches along each side. I felt quite inferior to Ilse and Elli. They both looked so good in shorts with their tans. I just don't tan. Also my legs are so skinny. Ilse said she couldn't go in to swim. I asked, 'Why?' and they looked at each other and then she said, 'I just can't.'"

I guess, in retrospect, that Ilse was having her period, and in the days before tampons couldn't go in the water. The sisters must have realized my naïveté and didn't want to enlighten me about these feminine matters. I suppose that my own menarche was delayed because of malnutrition and stress.

One day, a CARE package arrived from America. What a wonderful surprise! There were all kinds of goodies: flour, Crisco, chocolate, peanut butter, cookies, butter, sugar, and coffee. Klara loved the coffee. Gitte and Uli couldn't quite figure out what to do with the peanut butter. Then another month or so later, we received another CARE package.

I have had a soft spot in my heart for CARE ever since then and have been a regular contributor to this worthy organization for over sixty years now! I'm glad that the headquarters are right here in Atlanta, Georgia, where I now live. I am also glad that CARE's focus, although CARE packages still happen, now is to help women throughout the world. Improving the education of women and supporting their economic status results in fewer and healthier children, who will also become educated. As a result, women, children, and husbands all benefit.

I remember: Sometimes I practiced piano in the big recreation hall. One day, Hartmut's older brother, Lothar, came in. He didn't look anything like Hartmut. He was taller, dark, muscular, with a bit of beard stubble. He sat down at the piano when I'd finished and played. Wow! He could really play. He played Beethoven's Pathétique *with such deep emotion, plus great technique. Fabulous.*

*On another day, I was sitting on a tree behind our recreation hall and Lothar came walking by. He greeted me with a smile and I felt quite proud that he noticed me. I called out to him, "Come over here a minute!" and he approached. I taunted him, "I bet you can't climb that tree next to mine." He was a lot heavier than I, but he managed. He then smoked a cigarette. We talked about this and that and he asked me if I wanted to see a secret place. I agreed and he took me walking along the banks of the river Isar. There are lovely nooks, where weeping willows make little private tents. I kept standing as he sat down in one of those secret spots, and he looked up at me and said, "Now come on down here already and sit down." So I did and we talked again. I looked at my old black shoes with the pointed toes and hated how they looked. I twirled a ring out of a willow branch, and then, when Lothar pointed out what I was making, I was embarrassed and threw it into the water. Then I'd say something to provoke him, because he'd answer, "*Also, *Brigitte!" (Good grief, Brigitte!) in his Saxony dialect and I liked that. Well, he lay down next to me, turned over me, and held my arms up alongside my face. "Was soll ich jetzt mit dir machen?" (What am I going to do with you?) he asked. He rubbed his cheek softly against mine. I felt funny. In a way it was thrilling, but at the same time I was scared. "Get off me!" I said loudly as I jumped up. I stood on the bank above him and said, "You talked to me a lot just so you could smooch with me."*

On another occasion, when I was playing piano in the rec hall again, Lothar came in through a window. He stood behind me and helped me by putting his hands over mine. And yet another time he and his friend Klaus came through the ceiling trap door. Somehow, Lothar and I started a fight and Klaus just watched calmly and looked amused. But I noticed, as we were arm-wrestling, that Lothar kissed me on the forehead.

In the middle of summer, there was a festival in Landshut, commemorating a royal wedding in the Middle Ages. In the late afternoon, we teenagers walked from our apartment complex into town to the castle. There, in the inner courtyard, musicians assembled. We spectators lined the castle balconies. And then, as the full moon rose, we heard Mozart! The orchestra played Eine kleine Nachtmusik. *It was one of the loveliest experiences of my life. The music lingered in all of us as we quietly walked home along the beautiful Isar river.*

CHAPTER 15

1947: Life in Landshut with other prospective immigrants. April 1948: Ship voyage to America.

Klara wrote in Brigitte's album on October 27, 1947: "After a very hot and long summer, we now have fog and cold. Our furniture from Berlin has arrived, and now Brigitte can practice her piano here at home in our apartment. Papa writes that everything is going well. When will we be going on our big voyage? I've made a large Christmas package for Erich, including a long letter, illustrated by Brigitte and Ulrich. We have to send this parcel early."

I remember: During this time, we tried never to think of the terrible days of the war anymore. So many people were killed, wounded, or left homeless that the statistics exceed our human comprehension. Three million Germans died after VE Day, most in Soviet captivity. Some POWs were still held in 1979.

While we lived in Landshut, I remember one day in the fall vividly. I woke up with a bad tummy ache. I felt okay otherwise. Mutti had a friend over and they told me to lie down on the couch and skip school. It kept cramping in my lower abdomen and didn't get any better when I tried eating or when I drank the chamomile tea Mutti made me. Then, when I went to the bathroom in the early afternoon, I had a big scare: There was blood in the toilet! I called Mutti and she explained to me that I was having my first period. She got out a little packet with an information folder and a sanitary napkin that she had saved for me. She showed me how to put on the thin little elastic belt that held the napkin in place. But she also said, "It's very hard to get sanitary pads, so you have to put some toilet paper, wadded up, on top of the pad. That'll make it last longer." I later kept having periods irregularly, sometimes with cramps and sometimes not.

The experience of shortages of paper, pens and pencils, and toilet paper has had a lasting effect on me. I always have a cabinet full of toilet paper in the bathroom. And I have ridiculously large supplies of printer/copy paper, legal pads, notepads, file folders, pencils, pens, markers, and highlighters.

I wrote in a little diary booklet:

> I used to think that Lothar sort of made fun of me because I am younger than he, but now I believe that he actually liked me. Once we were in the dark corridor of the Miller's apartment, and he held me against the wall and tried to kiss me. Anyway, now he has a new girlfriend. She's tall and dark and has boring legs, with no shape to them.
>
> I'm more friends with his younger brother, Hartmut, now. He's my ideal—smart, talented, and very good looking. Clean cut, not only physically, but mentally. His hands are elegant and his writing is beautiful. He also plays piano well, and we've played a piano duet for school, and also once a piece with me on piano and him on violin.
>
> We just saw a movie together, *The Bells of St. Mary's*, with Bing Crosby and Ingrid Bergman. Once our elbows touched on the armrest between us. Wow! What an exciting and secret feeling that gave me. I didn't move. We were sitting way up high, where it was dark.
>
> We're all taking riding lessons now, in a big arena. I'm better, the Hungarian instructor says, because my posture is perfect. The horses are just so-so. We ride around in circles on a sand floor, learning dressage. My best girlfriend is Roswitha and we tell each other everything.
>
> Mutti is so worried about my heart that she doesn't want me to play strenuous ball games. I do get hot when I run in the heat, but I don't feel that anything else is wrong.

In early December, Klara wrote, "It's Advent. This whole time is uneasy for us. We're packing and waiting. In early November, we were told that it wouldn't be long now before we'll leave, and almost every day we send some boxes overseas. It's hard to get into the Christmas spirit, but I try. I've made the traditional Advent plate, with four candles and greens. On St. Nicholas's Day, December 5, the children each put a shoe on the windowsill, and the next morning they found them filled (with goodies from Papa). Will we be on board a ship on Christmas Day? May God bless our next steps."

Uli, age eleven, drew a pine branch with candle and ornaments into his sister's photo/life book and added, in pencil, "Soon we'll be going!" (*I added, "We've had two days' vacation, but now the schoolwork begins again. I'm happy that soon we'll be seeing our Papa again." I drew a little angel under my note.*)

On the next page in Brigitte's album there is a telegram, pasted in by Klara and now quite discolored: "Mrs. Klara Buchman, German Civil Housing Project, Landshut. Have house ready for you. Letter regarding furniture will follow. Will see you soon. Wish you, Uli, and Brigitte Merry Christmas. Love, Erich."

Under it, Klara wrote, "This was our greatest Christmas surprise, which fluttered into our home on December 26. We're supposed to leave about January 20!"

But, surprise, the next note by Klara in Brigitte's album is dated February 16, 1948, and reads: "We're still sitting here on the *Wartburg* [a play on words: the Wartburg is the castle where Martin Luther translated the New Testament from Greek into German; but *warten* also means to wait]. We're living in the midst of packed suitcases and boxes. Often we get angry and aggravated, but then I ask myself, 'We're in a warm apartment and have enough to eat; who else has that these days in our poor Germany?' And thus we forge ahead, practicing Christian patience. After all, there are quite a few families here in the same situation. We support each other with talks over coffee, trying to make a joke of it all. Sometimes Frl. Krumm comes by with Mr. Biemüller, and then we have a musical evening with recorder, lute, and singing."

I remember clearly: Frl. Liesel Krumm was a middle-aged former member of a hiking/singing group. She was sweet. (We would call her a former "hippie" these days.) She lived with Mr. Biemüller, who was quite a bit younger, but the same music/hiking/environment-loving type. Mutti liked them, but I could tell that she was uncomfortable with the idea that these two lived together, despite not being married and despite the age difference. However, Mutti overcame her bourgeois ideas because these two were such nice, helpful, and interesting people.

I also remember: Hartmut and I often went sledding in the hills together. The other afternoon we even went skiing. It was my first time. Hartmut was very nice. He carried a pair of long wooden skis for me and patiently showed me how to do everything. I was wearing Mutti's old sweat pants. After a while, I got the hang of it and enjoyed flying down the hill. Climbing up again was not so much fun. We stayed late, until the moon came up, looking quite reddish in the dark sky.

Klara continued writing into Brigitte's album: "It's early spring now and the sun's warmth and longer days make it a little easier to bear this difficult time of waiting and transition. Both children had good report cards from the camp school. Gitte attended a theater presentation with friends. Occasionally, we see a movie. But mostly we three read, which gives our lives daily adventures."

Brigitte wrote the next note in her album herself on April 4, 1948: "During the last few days, we were very bored and played ping-pong all day long in the rec room. They keep putting off the transport date and nobody tells us anything about why the delay. But today Mutti was lying on the sofa, reading a mystery, when a man came by with this little typewritten note, which I'm pasting in here:

Re: Departure of the next shipments

1. All persons scheduled for the next transport will be picked up from their quarters on Saturday, April 3, 1948, at 9:30 a.m. for a medical examination.
2. Saturday morning, all participants in the next shipments are to be available in

their quarters for an inspection of their carry-on luggage.

3. All participants of the next shipment are to be ready to be picked up on Monday, April 5, at 5:30 a.m.

"One of the girls was scared about the medical checkup because she had a sore throat, but the nurse just looked at her and checked for a skin rash and that was all. Now we're excited about tomorrow. This afternoon we will finish packing the suitcases, and then in the morning we go!"

I remember: We were now on our trip, waiting in a fancy hotel lobby somewhere. Mutti had dressed well, and Uli and I were wearing our best outfits and shoes and coats. Then some American women and children came in. I didn't like the way they looked. The women were wearing a lot of makeup, their hair was stiff, and their lipstick very red. Their nails were too long and red. And there was a little girl, maybe six, dressed in a blue velvet coat with a muff. It all looked too, too fancy, especially in Germany, where everything was gray and in ruins and people were starving.

Among the diaries, letters, and albums in my source boxes, I found a long, pencil-written booklet by my brother Uli, illustrated by me, describing our journey by ship to America. Here is a translation:

DESCRIPTION OF OUR TRIP TO AMERICA, April 6–16, 1948

By Ulrich (Uli) Buchmann, age eleven and a half

Our Trip from Germany to America

Finally, finally we're getting going, early in the morning at 5:30 a.m. Everything was already packed and ready to go. It was still quite dark when Herr Kähler knocked on our door. Soon Mutti, Gitte, and I, and the other twenty-two people, were on the bus. After about a half hour of saying our goodbyes we were driven to the train station. There we saw an *RTO* wagon *[I don't know what that was]*, which was coupled onto another train. That's the one we entered. Mutti, Gitte, and I had a compartment to ourselves, but the others also had compartments. Shortly after nine o'clock, the train left Landshut, to Bremerhaven!

On the trip, we played chess and other games. At noon, we were served an exquisite lunch in the dining car—not too much, but very good and pretty. We saw many big cities on the way. In the evening, we again had a yummy meal. Our compartment wasn't a sleeper, so space was tight, but we slept well anyway because we were dead tired.

The next morning, we arrived in Bremerhaven. It was April 6, 1948. After a lot of being moved back and forth, we were driven onto the pier (still in the train). The outside air smelled of the sea, wonderful. On the pier, we stopped. And there—hardly ten meters away from our train—was our ship, named *General R. E. Callan.* The others thought it was very small, but to me it seemed huge. It was 365 feet long and about 80 feet wide, but only 8,325 tons.

At ten o'clock, we entered the ship! Mutti and Gitte got a stateroom, number fifteen, all to themselves. That was nice, but it had no porthole and was hot and stuffy! That was not so nice. I got to sleep in the men's dormitory! That was a big hall with fifty others in the same room, but it was nice and cool. It was on 6 E. Hans and Paul (thirteen years and sixteen years) also slept there. They were my friends, and we were all going to America together. I slept on the top bunk with Hans, and Paul was below us.

It was a beautiful, warm day. The sea sparkled. There were many other large ships in the harbor. I explored our ship, up front, in back, upstairs, and downstairs. One could easily get lost. At noon, there was a humongous lunch, almost too good and too much. *[Note how important food was to us, especially my little brother.]* In the afternoon, several hundred Americans also came aboard.

Finally, finally, finally, in the afternoon, punctually at four o'clock, the *General Callan* blew its ship's horn three times with horrible loudness, so that the other ships almost sank with the fearful shock. And then we moved!

The deck was crammed full of people, and anyone who had a deck chair felt like a king. Two tugboats piloted us slowly and safely out of the harbor. Little by little, the deck emptied. In the evening again we got a tremendous, rich dinner. From now on, we always had enormous, good breakfasts, lunches, and dinners. We didn't go to bed 'til late, and Hans and I talked and joked around for a long time.

The next morning, we could already tell in the sleep dormitory that we were at sea. The ship rolled mightily. On deck, we saw that the waves were high. Then we saw land. Everyone thought it was England. But—was it? A compass had broken, and therefore the ship had sailed back during the night to Bremerhaven.

Now, soon, we left the harbor for the second time. When I visited Mutti and Gitte in their cabin, I found that they both were already seasick. They didn't want to go to the dining room. When I got there myself and smelled all the food, I got nauseous too. And many others also were seasick. By evening, most of us felt a little better. And so it went for the whole trip. Sometimes we were seasick and other times we felt okay. I was sick for about two days, Mutti for about three days, and Gitte four days. She was the most seasick.

I remember a nurse coming to our room and offering Mutti and me pineapple juice. That sweet juice made us even sicker.

The big object of each day was to fight for one of the deck chairs. Something funny happened one night during a lifesaving practice in a heavy storm. Two stowaways were found in one of the lifeboats. They must have smuggled themselves in during one of our two boardings. A seaman apparently gave them food every day. Now they were put into the ship's prison.

We children often played board games in the social parlor. There also was a library and a shop. We received ten dollars per family. Movies and books were free. Sometimes we saw flying fish, and once someone saw a whale or a shark. If it was foggy, our ship blew its whistle every five minutes. It was so terribly loud that the fish looked out of the water at us with wide, scared eyes. The ship often rolled and pitched something awful, and the waves were as high as houses.

The trip lasted nine days. During the last days, the seamen painted everything and oiled the ropes. And finally all the colorful flags were raised. Early on April 16, 1948, at 8:00 a.m., we saw land. At 9:00, the water seemed whitish, calm, and dirty, and there were a lot of seagulls flying around. The water got more and more dirty and we moved more and more slowly. At 9:45, two pilot tugboats came to guide our ship. At 10:15, we could already recognize everything on shore. We were moving terribly slowly. The deck was packed with people. There were many other big ships all around us. Everything was a lot like in Bremerhaven, except that it was much dirtier here.

At 10:30, we could disembark. First the Germans, then the Americans. Then onto the bus to Brooklyn. That looked a lot like Germany, only the stores, streets, and houses were quite different. "Eight oranges for five cents," it said everywhere; "Five bananas, five cents." Everything seemed to be available here. Most of our German families were brought to a hotel in Brooklyn; only two other families continued on with us. An officer was going to escort our three families to Washington. At about 3:00 p.m., we were driving through New York. The streets were full of little and large cars, bicycles, and buses. We drove over high bridges. From one high bridge, we even saw the Statue of Liberty. And we saw everything, everything one might like to buy. We even drove through Broadway, the main street of New York. Didn't see any skyscrapers, though [?]. At 3:20 p.m., we arrived at the train station. And here we three families were separated.

Now we entered a beautiful, carpeted Pullman train with tables and pretty, soft chairs. In the evening, at 6:45, we arrived in Washington. It was already dark outside, but we were surprised by the red, yellow, and other-color lights and advertisements; in other words, it was colorful everywhere.

In the train station, there was our Papa awaiting us! That was just terrific! After all the greetings were done, we were driven by a lady in a beautiful private car to our house. Everywhere we saw ads and lights and cars. We also passed the zoo. After an hour, we arrived at our house on Arden Road at Tomlinson Avenue, in Cabin John, Maryland, which is in a pretty neighborhood. It has a big yard, although it's somewhat away from the city. Now we were all happy. Hurray, hurray, now we've arrived!

I remember: Mutti didn't like the woman who came with Papa. I thought that Mutti was jealous and upset to see this woman with Papa. She was well dressed and wore lipstick and had a nice hairdo and acted very nice, but I could tell Mutti was mad to see her husband with another woman.

I wonder how my father fared during that year when he was alone in a new country with a new culture, and at a new job. He knew some English;

how quickly could he translate his knowledge at work? Where did he live? How did he commute where there was no public transportation and he did not yet have a car? How did he shop, eat, socialize? I don't remember hearing this discussed and I never thought to ask him. And now it's too late. How I wish I had become interested in family history sooner, when I could still have discussed with my parents the many questions that now come up!

I remember: We felt so good to be together again as a family. The house was pretty—two stories, white stucco, with exposed brick around the windows. We were happy to be in a country that was not destroyed, that had lots of food and opportunities for the future. We were all looking forward to our new adventures in America and grateful to be here.

wounds of a terrible war, but healed well enough to thrive and prosper."

"It made me wonder how I would cope if we were caught in a regime change to a fascist dictatorship and then a horrendous war."

"A great resource of primary source material for historians."

" Of interest to departments of German culture and history."

"This would be of interest to persons working on Women's Studies."

"Especially in the mother's notes and photos you can follow the enormous changes in women's fashions, from corsets and long dresses and hair and boots to short flapper dresses, compressing the breasts, and then back to mid-calf dresses emphasizing the bust. At the same time women began to work, got the vote and achieved higher education."

"We read here how this professional family started with bourgeois manners, transitioned to survival mode of obtaining food and fleeing bombed Berlin and later from the Russians, and then bravely faced a new future in a new country with new culture and language."

COMMENTS 1/17

Early readers said :

"I couldn't put the book down. I stayed up all night reading it."

"I started reading and reading and kept on and read it all the way through in one session."

"It's an interesting point of view of World War II from 'the other side', from the German side, the losing side, from a mother's side, coping with a disastrous unwanted war in a brave manner, from the children's side, coping in a naïve, matter-of-fact way, from the parents's side, trying to preserve family life.

The author's occasional insertion of historical events anchors the writings translated by the author from diaries, letters and photo albums."

"A retired physician, mother of three and grandmother of eight wrote this memoir as matriarch of her family in the United States to preserve family history. Having immigrated after the war, the family quickly integrated into American culture, worked

Poem in German and English

Kinderjahre-Ein Gedicht Bericht

Brigitte, ein kleines deutsches Mädchen,
Wächst auf in Kiel.
Als ihre Mutter schwanger war in 1932
Sah sie viele junge Männer sich lümmeln im Park.
Aber 1936, schwanger mit Brüderchen Ulrich,
Hatten die Männer Arbeit.
Schöne Wohnung in Kiel;
Papa Wissenschaftler, Mutti schreibt Artikel und Romane.
Kindermädchen, Strand und Park.

Papa befördert nach Berlin.
Wohnung in Spandau, nahe an der Havel.
Aber jetzt ist Krieg.
Sirenen, Fliegerangriffe, Bomben.
Schule unterbrochen, wenig Papier,
Bücher und Bleistifte knapp. Essen auch knapp.
Jede Nacht heult die Sirene, hoch und runter.
Aufstehen, anziehen, mit Köfferchen in den Luftschutzkeller.
Dann der lange Ton:Angriff vorüber.
Nie wissen, was wir oben finden:
Wohnung noch da, oder Trümmer?

Frauen und Kinder evakuiert aus Berliin.
Auf's Land zur Oma in Voerde.
Schön für die Kinder. Aber neue Schulen, keine Freunde.Nicht so leicht hier für Mutti.
Papa schickt eine Lebenszeichen-Karte
Nach jedem Luftangriff auf Berlin.

Wieder umgezogen in 1944, nach Bad Frankenhausen.
Kellerzimmer im Häuschen der "Tante" Liesl.
Neue Schule. Die Kinder hier sind wieder nicht freundlich.
Geschichte und Mathematik ganz durcheinander für uns.

Childhood Years—A Poem Report

Brigitte, a little German girl,
Grows up in Kiel.
When her mother was pregnant in 1932
She saw many young men loitering in the park.
But in 1936, pregnant with little brother Ulrich,
These men had work.
Nice apartment in Kiel;
Papa scientist, Mutti writes articles and novels.
Maid, beach, park.

Papa promoted to Berlin.
Apartment in Spandau, near the Havel river.
But now it is wartime.
Sirens, air raids, bombs.
School disrupted, shortage of paper,
Books and pencils. Food scarce.
Every night the siren howls with an up-and-down pitch.
We wake up, get dressed, go down
to the air raid shelter with our bags.
Then the long siren tone: the attack is over.
We never know what we'll find upstairs.
Is our home still there, or only ruin and debris?

Women and children evacuated from Berlin.
Into the countryside to Oma in Voerde.
Fun for the kids. But new schools, no friends. Not so easy here for Mutti.
Papa sends a "sign of life" postcard
After each air raid over Berlin.

We've moved again in 1944, to Bad Frankenhausen.
Two basement rooms in "Auntie" Liesl's small house.
New school. The kids here again are not friendly.
Confused in history and math.

Wenig zu essen.
Eines Tages ein langer, langer Sirenenton:
Die Amerikaner sind hier.
Der Krieg ist vorüber!
Schwarze mit weissen Zähnen und Hershey bars.
Doch plötzlich müssen wir wieder fliehen. Die Russen kommen.
Offener Lastwagen durch Deutschland zum Norden.
Ueberall zerstörte Städte.
Uebernachten in einer Scheune. Später Läuse.

Lager für Wissenschaftler unter britischer Kontrolle
Im schönen Dänisch-Nienhof. Ostsee und Strand.
Steilküste, Buchenwald, Pilze.
Brigitte züchtet Kaninchen: Fleisch für sonntags.
Papa nimmt Vertrag nach Amerika an.

Umgezogen auf ein Jahr nach Landshut an der Isar.
Dom und Burg. Privatstunden.
Brigitte entdeckt Jungen.

Endlich nach Amerika, 1948.
Cabin John, Maryland, nahe Washington, DC.
Bethesda-Chevy Chase High School.
Vom Kriegskind zum typischen Teenager
Mit boyfriend in einem Jahr!

Little to eat.
One day a long, long, steady siren tone:
The Americans are here.
The war is over!
Black soldiers with white teeth and Hershey bars.
But suddenly we have to flee again.
The Russians are coming.
Open pickup truck through destroyed Germany
To the north.
Overnight in barn. Later, lice.

Camp for scientists under British command
In beautiful Dänisch-Nienhof.
Blue Baltic Sea and beach, cliffs,
Beech woods, mushrooms, and berries.
Brigitte raises rabbits: meat for Sundays.
Papa signs contract to go to America.

Moving again, for a year to Landshut an der Isar.
Cathedral and castle. Private lessons.
Brigitte discovers boys.

Finally arriving in America, 1948.
Cabin John, Maryland, near Washington, DC.
Bethesda-Chevy Chase High School.
From German war waif to typical American teenager
With boyfriend in one year!

Additional Reading

Anonymous. *A Woman in Berlin: Eight Weeks in the Conquered City*. New York: Henry Holt and Company, 2000.

Beschloss, Michael. *The Conquerors*. New York: Simon and Schuster, 2002.

Bessel, Richard. *Germany 1945: From War to Peace*. New York: HarperCollins, 2010.

Bilger, Burkhard. "Where Germans Make Peace with Their Dead." *The New Yorker*, September 12, 2016: 56–68.

Bohjalian, Chris. *Skeletons at the Feast*. New York: Crown Publishing Group, 2008.

Bonhoeffer, Dietrich. *Widerstand und Ergebung*. München und Hamburg: Siebenstern Taschenbuch Verlag, 1951.

Bradley, Ernestine. *The Way Home: A German Childhood, an American Life*. New York: Pantheon Books, 2005.

Buchman, Frank N. D. *Remaking the World*. New York: Robert M. McBride and Company, 1949.

Busch, Wilhelm. *Max und Moritz*. Berlin: Braun Publisher, 1868.

Chang, Iris. *The Rape of Nanking: The Forgotten Holocaust of World War II*. New York: Perseus Books, 1997.

Childers, Thomas. *A History of Hitler's Empire*. Chantilly, VA: The Teaching Company Limited Partnership, 2001.

Clarke, Anna. *Last Voyage*. New York: Berkeley Publishing Group, 1980.

Dershowitz, Alan M. *Abraham: The World's First (But Certainly Not Last) Jewish Lawyer*. New York: Penguin Random House, 2015.

De Zayas, Alfred-Maurice. *A Terrible Revenge: The Ethnic Cleansing of the East European Germans*. New York: Macmillan, 2006.

Doerr, Anthony. *All the Light We Cannot See*. New York: Scribner, 2014.

Döscher, Hans-Jürgen. *Reichskristallnacht*. Hamburg: Zeitgeschichte, 1987.

Fest, Joachim. *Not I: Memoirs of a German Childhood*. Translated by Martin Chalmers. New York: Other Press, 2014.

Flood, Charles Bracelen. *Hitler: The Path to Power*. Boston: Houghton Mifflin Company, 1989.

Follett, Ken. *Winter of the World*. New York: Penguin Group, 2012.

Frank, Anne. *Anne Frank: The Diary of a Young Girl*. Translated by B. M. Mooyaart. New York: Doubleday, 1993.

Ghosts of the Baltic Sea. DVD. Directed by Jon Goodman. New York: Wellspring Media, 2006.

Goldsmith, Martin. *The Inextinguishable Symphony: A True Story of Music and Love in Nazi Germany*. New York: John Wiley and Sons, Inc., 2000.

Graf, Hildegard. *Ja Ja Mein Kind: Autobiography of a German Girl Who Lived Through the Second World War in Berlin*. n.p.: n.p., 1989.

Grass, Günter. *My Century*. Orlando: Harcourt, Inc., 1999.

Haman, Anna Louise. *War Victims: A German Family's Story of Confronting Social Normalcy*. Santa Fe: Nuevo Peace Publishing, 2011.

Hegi, Ursula. *Stones from the River*. New York: Scribner, 1997.

Hegi, Ursula. *Tearing the Silence: On Being German in America*. New York: Scribner, 1997.

Heiligenpahl, Günter. *Ehre sei den wackeren Brünern*. Fürth, Ger.: Brüner Bürgerverein, 1982.

Heisenberg, Werner. *Physics and Beyond: Encounters and Conversations*. New York: Harper & Row, Publishers, Inc., 1971.

Howard, Peter. *Frank Buchman's Secret*. New York: Doubleday, 1962.

Huber, Sonya. *Opa Nobody*. Lincoln, NE: University of Nebraska Press, 2008.

Jacobsen, Annie. *Operation Paperclip*. New York: Little, Brown and Company, 2014.

Kanon, Joseph. *The Good German*. New York: Henry Holt and Co., 2001.

Kolbert, Elizabeth. "The Last Trial: A Great-Grandmother, Auschwitz, and the Arc of Justice." *The New Yorker*, February 16, 2015.

Larson, Erik. *In the Garden of Beasts: Love, Terror, and an American Family in Hitler's Berlin*. New York: Penguin Random House, 2011.

Lorant, Stefan. *SIEG HEIL (HAIL TO VICTORY): An Illustrated History of Germany from Bismarck to Hitler*. New York: W. W. Norton & Company, 1974.

Lorenz, Hilke. *Kriegskinder: Das Schicksal einer Generation*. Berlin: Ullstein Buchverlage, 2002.

MacRae, Sigrid. *A World Elsewhere: An American Woman in Wartime Germany*. New York: Penguin Group, 2015.

Marsh, Charles. *Strange Glory: A Life of Dietrich Bonhoeffer*. New York: Knopf, 2014.

Mishra, Pankaj. "Land and Blood: The Origins of the Second World War in Asia." *The New Yorker*, November 25, 2013.

Nahmias, Brigitte. "Haiku." In *Gedichte und Erinnerungen*, 45. Athens, GA: *Das Fenster* (2010).

———. "Kinderjahre." In *Gedichte und Erinnerungen*, 118–19. Athens, GA: *Das Fenster* (2010).

———. "Willie: A Character Sketch," in *Onward! Bard's Book: A Teacher's Legacy*. Cumming, GA: Brandywine Printing, Inc. (2010), 232–237.

———. "The Wisdom Mountain: An Identity Poem." In *Inner Lives: Women Writers Explore Their Identity, Expression, and Transformation* by UUCA Women Writers. Alpharetta, GA: BookLogix (2011), 37–39.

———. *Widdely, the Naughty Little Angel*. Alpharetta, GA: BookLogix (2014).

Nossack, Hans Erich. *The End: Hamburg 1943.*Translated and with a new foreword by Joel Agee. Chicago: The University of Chicago Press, 2004.

Petersen, Christa. *Iron Henry: A Child's Account of World War II*. Norcross, GA: Christa Petersen, 2003.

Prauser, Hans-Joachim. *Unforeseen*. Virginia Beach, VA: Hans-Joachim Prauser, 2013.

Reader's Digest Illustrated Story of World War II. Pleasantville, NY: The Reader's Digest Association, Inc., 1969.

Schemm, Hans. *Born on a Sunday.* Denver: Acorn Publishing, 2004.

Schwartz, Mimi. *Good Neighbors, Bad Times: Echoes of my Father's German Village.* Lincoln, NE: University of Nebraska Press, 2009.

Segre, Gino. *Faust in Copenhagen.* New York: Penguin Group, 2007.

Sepetys, Ruta. *Between Shades of Gray.* New York: Penguin Group, 2011.

Shirer, William L. *The Rise and Fall of the Third Reich.* New York: Ballantine Books, 1959.

Sifton, Elisabeth. *The Serenity Prayer.* New York: W. W. Norton and Company, 2003.

Special 1945–1948 issue, *SPIEGEL* 4 (1995).

Stargardt, Nicholas. *A Nation Under Arms, 1939–1945.* New York: Perseus Books, 2015.

Strickland, Eyke. *Eyes are Watching, Ears are Listening: Growing up in Nazi Germany 1933–1946.* New York: iUniverse, Inc., 2008.

Sulzberger, C. L. *The American Heritage Picture History of World War II.* Rockville, MD: American Heritage Publishing Co., Inc., 1966.

Weber, Thomas. *Wie Adolf Hitler zum Nazi wurde.* Berlin: Propyläen Verlag, 2016.

Wesley, Mary. *The Camomile Lawn.* London: Macmillan, 1984.

Zusak, Markus. *The Book Thief.* New York: Alfred A. Knopf, 2005.

About the Author

Brigitte "Bee" Buchmann Nahmias, MD, began writing this memoir about her childhood in Germany for her family in the United States, but soon many early reviewers also expressed great interest in the historical aspects.

In 1948, three years after the war ended, she moved with her family to the Washington, DC, area. She was fifteen. Brigitte and her brother, Ulrich, both became doctors. Brigitte attended Bethesda Chevy-Chase High School, won a scholarship to George Washington University in DC, and then attended GW School of Medicine. Here she met and married her classmate, Andre Nahmias, a Sephardic Jewish immigrant from Alexandria, Egypt. The couple moved to Atlanta, Georgia, and had three children, Cindy, David, and Eddy. Dr. Nahmias was director of a regional emphysema clinic, affiliated with St. Joseph's Infirmary; assistant clinical professor of medicine and director of Emory University Medical Television; clinician at Fulton County Health Department; and president of her own company, Medical

Video Productions. She also was a dedicated soccer mom, PTA president, and active in the UUCA (Unitarian Universalist Congregation of Atlanta).

She later married a classical musician, Dr. Donald Norton.

Since retirement, Dr. Nahmias enjoys playing piano and recorders and has played with many groups. She also likes reading, painting, and gardening, and supports many environmental causes. But most of all, she loves her eight grandchildren and many get-togethers with her friends.